CHORAL SCORES

CHORAL SCORES

EDITED BY

DENNIS SHROCK

OXFORD
UNIVERSITY PRESS

OXFORD

UNIVERSITY PRESS

Oxford University Press is a department of the University of
Oxford. It furthers the University's objective of excellence in research,
scholarship, and education by publishing worldwide.

Oxford   New York
Auckland   Cape Town   Dar es Salaam   Hong Kong   Karachi
Kuala Lumpur   Madrid   Melbourne   Mexico City   Nairobi
New Delhi   Shanghai   Taipei   Toronto

With offices in
Argentina   Austria   Brazil   Chile   Czech Republic   France   Greece
Guatemala   Hungary   Italy   Japan   Poland   Portugal   Singapore
South Korea   Switzerland   Thailand   Turkey   Ukraine   Vietnam

Oxford University Press
198 Madison Avenue, New York, NY 10016

ISBN 978-0-19-978189-8
ISBN 978-0-19-978190-4 (pbk.)

Contents

THE BAROQUE ERA

THE CLASSICAL ERA

THE ROMANTIC ERA

THE MODERN ERA

Acknowledgments

I am grateful to the following people, all of whom aided me tremendously during the process of compiling and editing this anthology and formatting many of the editions.

Bruce Mayhall, who researched, carefully edited, and set many of the choral/orchestral scores, including those by Bach, Mozart, Rossini, Berlioz, Fauré, Verdi, Mendelssohn, Brahms, and Boulanger, and who helped me reason through many of the issues that determined the anthology's outcome.

Ng Tian Hui, who first taught me the computer program for setting scores, who edited and set the Padilla and Jerusalem editions, and who worked with publishers to procure rights for the printing of modern editions.

Kyle Roderick, who frequently and generously helped me solve formatting issues.

Ryan Chatterton, who also generously helped me with computer issues and who set the Tormis, Howells, Britten, Tavener, Ives, Persichetti, and Pinkham scores.

Jason Bishop, who edited and set the Hildegard von Bingen chant and who helped me with Latin translations.

INTRODUCTION

The scores in this anthology have been chosen as illustrative examples of the major composers and their repertoire presented and discussed in *Choral Repertoire*, published by Oxford University Press in 2009. Scores have also been chosen to represent standard and customarily performed genres, such as mass, oratorio, madrigal, and part song (all of which are listed in the appendix). The choice of scores from the Medieval through the Romantic era has been based on the acknowledged importance of the composer and repertoire and the elucidative value of the music in terms of style (the representation of its genre) and structure (the noteworthiness of its formal characteristics). Otherwise, lesser-known but artistically superior works were chosen over popular and well-known works, and works were chosen that are not commonly represented in other anthologies. The choice of Modern-era scores has been dictated partly by publisher permission. Most publishers have been extremely cooperative. However, inclusion of some notable works has been impossible because publisher rights have been denied.

The organization of the anthology reflects that of the repertoire book—scores are presented chronologically according to historical era, then by country within the era, and, finally, in order of the composer's date of birth. Each score is either a complete composition, without abridgements or alterations, or an entire movement from a larger work. There are no open-ended excerpts of pieces or works. Furthermore, all scores are presented with their complete distribution of vocal and instrumental parts; no textures have been reduced to keyboard arrangements (except for the Persichetti and Pinkham pieces, which have composer-written piano accompaniments as alternative performance options), and no figured bass lines have been realized.

Being an anthology for study, not performance, there are also no keyboard reductions of orchestral or vocal scoring—those normally used for rehearsal purposes—and there are no syllabic slur marks, especially in repertoire before the Romantic era; slur marks have generally been retained as articulation symbols. Furthermore, there are no lines signifying word extensions, and tempo and expression marks are occasionally printed only in the top part of music rather than in all parts—these procedures being adopted in order to make the scores easier to read. Spelling has been modernized for consistency and comprehensibility.

Commentary about each score, mostly addressing issues of structure and identification of salient characteristics, appears in the appendix. Along with the commentary is the source of the score's text, if known, and a literal English translation of foreign-language texts. Biographical material about composers and historical information about scores can be found in *Choral Repertoire*.

Each score is presented according to the most current scholarly research. For repertoire from the Medieval and Renaissance eras, this involves careful attention to mensuration, key signatures, text underlay, and musica recta and ficta. In terms of mensuration, measure bars have been used to demarcate the regular flow of rhythm indicated by the original mensuration signs or meter signatures. This occasionally creates rhythmic syncopation, which was commonly mentioned as a positive compositional trait in primary sources of the Renaissance era. (See examples of syncopation in Lasso's *Tutto lo dì*, measures 17–19, and Sweelinck's *Or sus, serviteurs du Seigneur*, soprano part, measures 4–6.) Also, mensuration signs have been translated into modern signatures according to original meanings of tempus and prolation. For example, Dunstable's *Quam pulcra es* is printed here with 3/2 and 6/4 meters since the original manuscript has mensuration signs that indicate, first, a perfect tempus and an imperfect prolation, and later (measure 39), an imperfect tempus and a perfect prolation.

Key signatures have been chosen to fall within the boundaries of original clefs. With this in mind, note that the Tallis *If ye love me* is scored here for ATTB voices, not SATB as commonly seen in modern-day editions, and that Tomkins's *O pray for the peace of Jerusalem* is scored for SSTB, not SATB. Note also that many of the alto parts in the Renaissance-era editions are low since they were written for male altos, who have a lower range than female altos.

In terms of text underlay, Verdelot's *Italia mia* is printed here following Renaissance-era practices, not modern-day "come scritto" procedures. And Dufay's Kyrie from his *Missa L'homme armé* takes into consideration practices of both musica ficta (the F-sharps) and musica recta (the E-flats).

For repertoire from the Baroque and Classical eras, facsimiles of original scores have been consulted, with composer markings incorporated in the editions here when the markings have been thought to be instructive. For example, the movements from J. S. Bach's *B Minor Mass* and *St. John Passion* contain vocal slurrings found in Bach's autograph manuscript. Attention has also been given to performance practice issues of rhythmic alteration (e.g., see the Sanctus from Alessandro Scarlatti's *Messa di S Cecilia*) and ornamentation (e.g., see the cadential trills in the "Et incarnatus est" from Vivaldi's *Gloria* RV589 and "How excellent thy name, O Lord" from Handel's *Saul*). All editorial suggestions are marked above the staff in parentheses.

Each score throughout the anthology has been presented according to the most recent availability of scholarly editions, and many decisions about scoring, articulation, and dynamic markings are the result of comparisons between historic publications. As examples, the J. S. Bach *B Minor Mass* score here has taken into consideration the 2010 Bärenreiter edition of the Neue Bach Ausgabe as well as Bach's autograph score; the Mozart *Requiem* edition is the result of comparisons between the Mozart autograph, the Süssmayr autograph, and the Neue Mozart Ausgabe score; the Haydn *Creation* has considered the 1804 first published score along with the 1995 Oxford University Press score edited by A. Peter Brown; the Brahms *Requiem* contains ritardando signs (in the shape of a sideways S) found in the composer's conducting score; and the Fauré *Requiem* has considered the 1900 Hamelle publication, the 1983 Hinshaw edition edited by John Rutter, and original orchestral parts. The source or sources for each edition here can be found in the appendix.

THE MEDIEVAL ERA

1. Salve regina

Edited by Dennis Shrock

Anonymous

Sal - ve, re - gi - na, ma-ter mi - se - ri - cor-di - ae: vi - ta,

dul - ce - do, et spes no-stra, sal - ve. Ad te cla-ma-mus, ex-su-les,

fi - li - i He - vae; ad te sus-pi-ra - mus, ge-men-tes et flen - tes

in hac lac - ri-ma-rum val - le. E - ia er - go, ad-vo-ca - ta nos-tra,

il-los tu - os mi-se-ri-cor - des oc - u-los ad nos con - ver - te.

Et Je - sum, be - ne - dic - tum fruc-tum ven - tris tu - i, no - bis

post hoc ex-si-li - um os - ten-de. O cle - mens,

O pi - a, O dul-cis vir-go Ma-ri - a.

2. O viridissima virga

Edited by D. Jason Bishop

Hildegard von Bingen

O vi - ri - dis - si - ma vir - ga a - ve, que in ven-

- to - so fla - bro scis - ci - ta - ti - o - nis sanc - to - rum

pro - di - sti. Cum ve - nit tem - pus quod tu flo - ru -

-is - ti in ra - mis tu - is; a - ve, a - ve sit

ti - bi, qui - a ca - lor so - lis in te su - da - vit si - cut

o - dor bal - sa - mi. Nam in te

flo - ru - it pul - cher flos qui o - do - rem de - dit om - ni - bus a-

ro - ma - ti - bus que a - ri - da e - rant. Et il-

- la ap - pa - ru - e - runt om - ni - a in vi - ri - di - ta - te ple -

- - - na. Un - de ce - li de - de - runt ro - rem

su - per gra - men et om - nis ter - ra le - ta fac - ta est, quo - ni -

am vis - ce - ra ip - si - us fru - men - tum pro - tu - le - runt, et quo - ni -

am vo - lu - cres ce - li ni - dos in ip - sa ha - bu -

e - - runt. De - in - de fac - ta est es - ca ho - mi -

- ni - bus, et gau - di - um mag - num e - pu - lan - ti - um; un -

de, o sua - vis vir - go, in te non de - fi -

- cit ul - lum gau - - di - um. Hec om - ni -

- a E - va con - temp - sit. Nunc au - tem laus

sit al - - - - tis - si - mo.

3. Messe de nostre dame
Kyrie

Edited by Dennis Shrock

Guillaume de Machaut

4. Venecie, mundi splendor /
Michael, qui Stena domus / Italie, mundicie

Edited by Dennis Shrock

Johannes Ciconia

5. Quam pulcra es

Edited by Dennis Shrock

John Dunstable

Alto: Quam pul - cra es et quam de - co - ra, ca -

Tenor: Quam pul - cra es et quam de - co - ra, ca -

Bass: Quam pul - cra es et quam de - co - ra, ca -

A.: ris - si - ma in de - li - - - ci - is. Sta -

T.: ris - si - ma in de - li - - - ci - is. Sta -

B.: ris - si - ma in de - li - - - ci - is. Sta -

A.: tu - ra tu - a as - si - mi - la - ta est pal - -

T.: tu - ra tu - a as - si - mi - la - ta est pal - -

B.: tu - ra tu - a a - si - mi - la - ta est pal - -

A.: me, et u - be - ra tu - a bo - tris. Ca - put tu -

T.: me, et u - be - ra tu - a bo - tris. Ca - put tu -

B.: me, et u - be - ra tu - a bo - tris. Ca - put tu -

20

A. um ut Car - me - lus, col - lum tu - um

T. um ut Car - me - lus, col - lum tu - um

B. um ut Car - - me - lus, col - lum tu - um

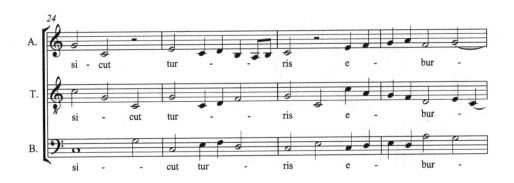

24

A. si - cut tur - - ris e - bur -

T. si - cut tur - - ris e - bur -

B. si - - cut tur - ris e - bur

28

A. - - ne - a. Ve - -

T. - - ne - a. Ve - -

B. - - ne - a. Ve - -

32

A. ni, di - le - - cte mi, e - gre - di - a -

T. ni, di - le - - cte mi, e - gre - di - a -

B. ni, di - le - - cte mi, e - gre - di - a -

THE RENAISSANCE ERA

6. Missa L'homme armé
Kyrie

Edited by Dennis Shrock

Guillaume Dufay

7. Missa de beata virgine
Agnus Dei

Edited by Dennis Shrock   Josquin Desprez

8. Au joli jeu

Edited by Dennis Shrock

Clément Janequin

9. Ainsi qu'on oit le cerf bruire

Edited by Dennis Shrock

Claude Goudimel

Soprano: Ain - si qu'on oit le cerf brui - re, pour - chas-sant le frais des eaux;

Alto: Ain - si qu'on oit le cerf brui - re, pour - chas-sant le frais des eaux;

Tenor: Ain - si qu'on oit le cerf brui - re, pour - chas-sant le frais des eaux;

Bass: Ain - si qu'on oit le cerf brui - re, pour - chas-sant le frais des eaux;

S. ain - si mon coeur qui sou - pi - re, Sei - gneur, a - près tes rui - seaux.

A. ain - si mon coeur qui sou - pi - re, Sei - gneur, a - près tes rui - seaux.

T. ain - si mon coeur qui sou - pi - re, Sei - gneur, a - près tes rui - seaux.

B. ain - si mon coeur qui sou - pi - re, Sei - gneur, a - près tes rui - seaux.

S. Va tous - jours cri - ant, sui - vant, le grand, le grand Dieu vi - vant, hé - las don -

A. Va tou - jours cri - ant, sui - vant, le grand, le grand Dieu vi - vant, hé - las don -

T. Va tou - jours cri - ant, sui - vant, le grand, le grand Dieu vi - vant, hé - las don -

B. Va tou - jours cri - ant, sui - vant, le grand, le grand Dieu vi - vant, hé - las don -

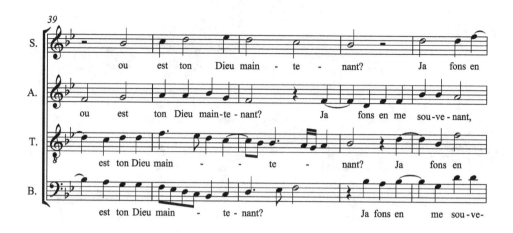

10. Amour cruel que pense tu

Edited by Dennis Shrock

Claude Le Jeune

11. Or sus, serviteurs du Seigneur

Edited by Dennis Shrock

Jan Pieterszoon Sweelinck

12. Italia mia

Edited by Dennis Shrock

Philippe Verdelot

13. Io dico che fra voi

Edited by Dennis Shrock

Jacques Arcadelt

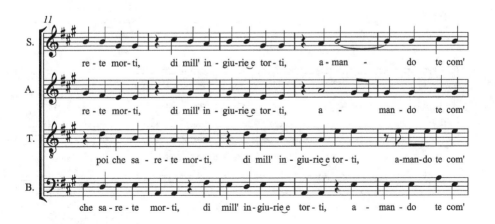

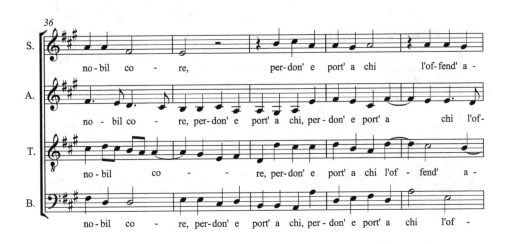

14. Ancor che col partire

Edited by Dennis Shrock

Cipriano de Rore

15. Tu es Petrus - Quodcumque ligaveris

Edited by Dennis Shrock

Giovanni Pierluigi da Palestrina

16. Missa Tu es Petrus

Kyrie

Edited by Dennis Shrock

Giovanni Pierluigi da Palestrina

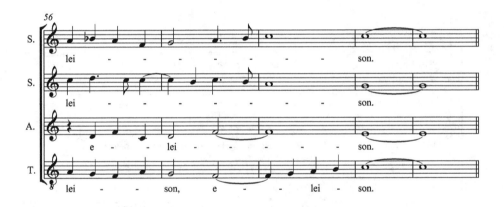

17. Fa una canzona

Edited by Dennis Shrock

Orazio Vecchi

18. Leggiadre ninfe

Edited by Dennis Shrock

Luca Marenzio

19. Amor vittorioso

Edited by Dennis Shrock

Giovanni Giacomo Gastoldi

20. Hodie Christus natus est

Edited by Dennis Shrock

Giovanni Gabrieli

21. Resta di darmi noia

Edited by Dennis Shrock

Carlo Gesualdo

22. Magnificat primi toni
Anima mea

Edited by Dennis Shrock   Cristóbal de Morales

23. A un niño llorando

Edited by Dennis Shrock

Francisco Guerrero

nos,   vi - da,   glo - - ria y cie - lo.

rei - nos,   vi - da,   glo - ria y cie - lo.

vi - da,   glo - ria y cie - - lo.

rei - nos,   vi - da,   glo - ria y   cie - lo.

nos,   vi - da,   glo - ria y   cie - lo.

2. Na - ce con tan - ta ba - je - za,   aun - que es
4. Al - ma, ve - nid tam - bién vos,   a a - do -

po - de - ro - so rey,   por - que nos da ya   por
rar tan al - to nom - bre ve - réis que es - te ni - ño es

ley   a - ba - ti - mien - to y po - bre - za.
hom - bre   y ma - yo - raz - go   de Dios.

24. Vere languores nostros

Edited by Dennis Shrock

Tomás Luis de Victoria

25. Innsbruck, ich muss dich lassen

Edited by Dennis Shrock

Heinrich Isaac

26. Musica Dei donum optimi

Edited by Dennis Shrock

Orlando di Lasso

27. Tutto lo dì

Edited by Dennis Shrock

Orlando di Lasso

28. Pater noster

Edited by Dennis Shrock

Jacob Handl

29. Dixit Maria

Edited by Dennis Shrock

Hans Leo Hassler

30. Es ist ein Ros entsprungen

Edited by Dennis Shrock

Michael Praetorius

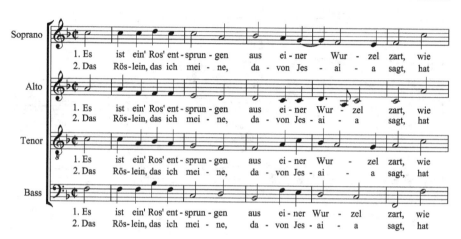

1. Es ist ein' Ros' ent-sprun-gen aus ei - ner Wur - zel zart, wie
2. Das Rös-lein, das ich mei - ne, da - von Jes - ai - a sagt, hat

uns die Al-ten sun - gen, von Jes - se kam die Art; und hat ein Blüm-lein
uns ge-bracht al - lei - ne Ma - rie, die rei - ne Magd; aus Got-tes ev' - gem

'bracht mit - ten im kal-ten Win - ter, wohl zu der hal - ben Nacht.
Rat, hat sie ein Kind ge - bo - ren blei - bend ein rei - ne Magd.

31. Meine Schwester, liebe Braut

Edited by Dennis Shrock

Melchior Franck

32. If ye love me

Edited by Dennis Shrock

Thomas Tallis

33. Ave verum corpus

Edited by Dennis Shrock

William Byrd

34. My bonny lass she smileth

Edited by Dennis Shrock

Thomas Morley

35. Now, oh now, I needs must part

Edited by Dennis Shrock

John Dowland

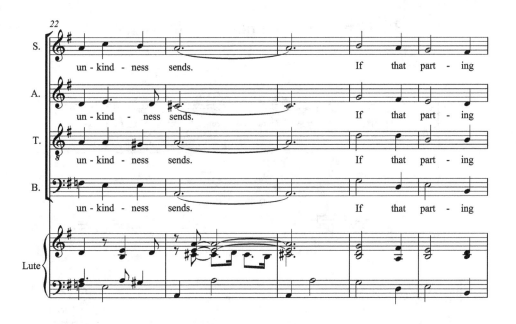

36. O pray for the peace of Jerusalem

Edited by Dennis Shrock

Thomas Tomkins

37. Flora gave me fairest flowers

Edited by Dennis Shrock

John Wilbye

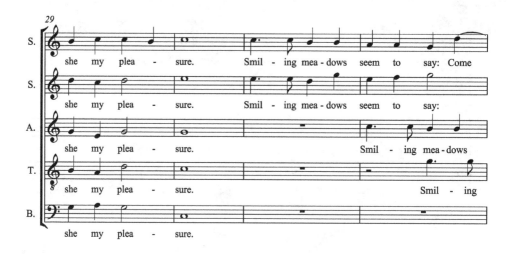

38. When David heard that Absalom was slain

Edited by Dennis Shrock

Thomas Weelkes

39. Almighty and everlasting God

Edited by Dennis Shrock

Orlando Gibbons

THE BAROQUE ERA

40. Confitebor secondo

Edited by Dennis Shrock

Claudio Monteverdi

41. Sfogava con le stelle

Edited by Dennis Shrock

Claudio Monteverdi

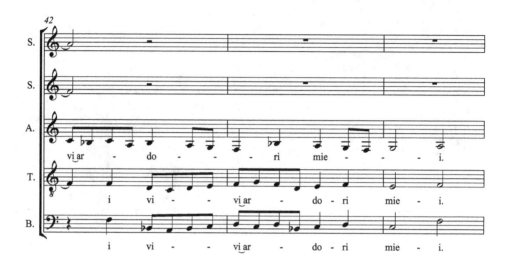

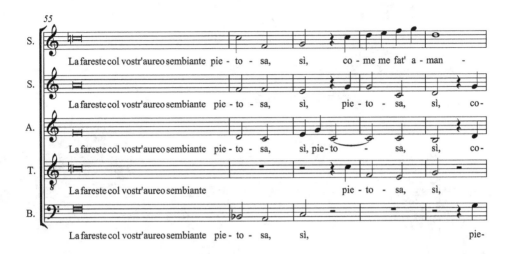

42. Jonas
Peccavimus Domine

Edited by Dennis Shrock

Giacomo Carissimi

43. Messa di S Cecilia
Sanctus

Edited by Dennis Shrock

Alessandro Scarlatti

44. Crucifixus

Edited by Dennis Shrock

Antonio Lotti

45. Gloria
RV589
Et in terra pax

Edited by Dennis Shrock

Antonio Vivaldi

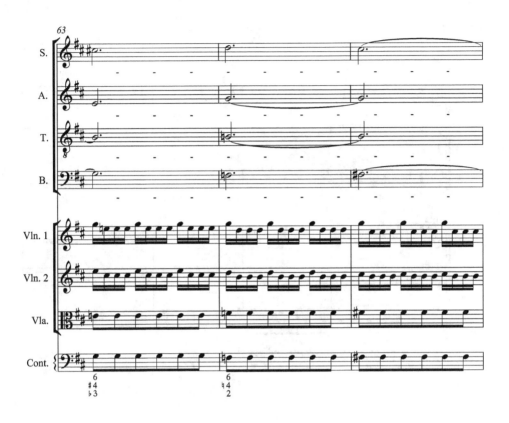

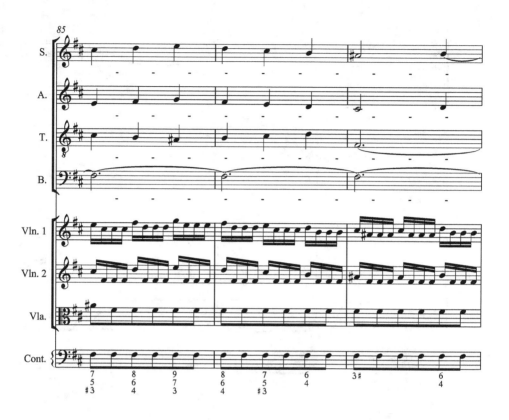

46. In nativitatem Domini canticum
H314

Edited by Dennis Shrock

Marc-Antoine Charpentier

Quem vi-di - stis, pa - sto-res, di - ci-te, an-nun-ci-

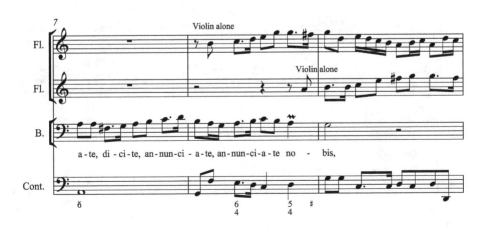

a - te, di - ci-te, an-nun-ci - a-te, an-nun-ci-a-te no - bis,

in ter-ra quis ap - pa - ru- it, di - ci-te, pa - sto-res, di - ci-te, an - nun - ci-

a - te, di - ci-te, an - nun - ci - a - te no - bis, di - ci-te, an - nun - ci - a - te no -

bis.

la - vit, re - ve - la - vit in ter - ra ju - sti - ti - am su - am, re - ve-

la - vit, re - ve - la - vit in ter - ra ju - sti - ti - am su - am.

Psal-li-te, psal-li-te Do - mi - no, psal-li-te Do - mi - no in ci - tha - ra,

Psal-li-te, psal-li-te Do - mi - no in ci - tha - ra,

Psal-li-te, psal-li-te Do - mi - no in ci - tha - ra,

Psal-li-te, psal-li-te Do - mi - no, psal-li-te Do - mi - no in ci - tha - ra,

47. Super flumina Babylonis
Hymnum cantate nobis

Edited by Dennis Shrock   Michel-Richard de Lalande

48. Musicalische Exequien
Herr, wenn ich nur dich habe

Edited by Dennis Shrock

Heinrich Schütz

49. Angelus ad pastores ait
SSWV13

Edited by Dennis Shrock

Samuel Scheidt

o vo - bis, an-nun-ci-o vo - bis, an-nun-ci-

an-nun-ci-o vo - bis, an-nun-ci-o vo - bis,

o vo-bis, an-nun-ci-o vo-bis, vo - bis, vo - bis,

an-nun-ci-o vo-bis, an-nun-ci-o vo-bis, vo - bis,

50. Das neugebor'ne Kindelein
BuxWV13

Edited by Dennis Shrock

Dietrich Buxtehude

51. Das ist meine Freude

Edited by Dennis Shrock

Johann Ludwig Bach

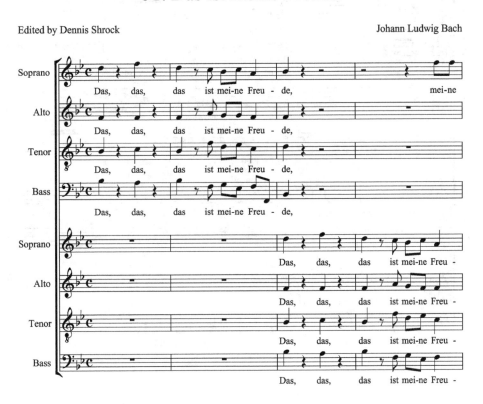

52. Uns ist ein Kind geboren
TWV1:1451
Movement 1

Edited by Dennis Shrock

Georg Philipp Telemann

53a. B Minor Mass
Et incarnatus est

Edited by Bruce Mayhall Rastrelli

Johann Sebastian Bach

53b. B Minor Mass
Crucifixus

Edited by Bruce Mayhall Rastrelli

Johann Sebastian Bach

53c. B Minor Mass
Et resurrexit

Edited by Bruce Mayhall Rastrelli

Johann Sebastian Bach

54a. Passio secundum Johannen
Ruht wohl

Edited by Bruce Mayhall Rastrelli

Johann Sebastian Bach

und bringt auch mich, und bringt auch mich zur Ruh, und bringt auch

und bringt auch mich zur Ruh, zur Ruh, und bringt auch

und bringt auch mich zur Ruh, und bringt auch

wohl und bringt auch mich zur Ruh, und bringt auch

mich zur Ruh! Das Grab, so euch be - stim -

mich zur Ruh! Das Grab, so euch be - stim -

mich zur Ruh! Das Grab, so euch be -

mich zur Ruh!

54b. Passio secundum Johannen

Ach Herr, lass dein lieb Engelein

Edited by Bruce Mayhall Rastrelli

Johann Sebastian Bach

Soprano [Flute 1 Oboe 1 Violin 1]
Ach Herr, lass dein lieb En - ge - lein am letz - ten End die
den Leib in seim Schlaf - käm - mer - lein gar sanft ohn ein - ge

Alto [Flute 2 Oboe 2 Violin 2]
Ach Herr, lass dein lieb En - ge - lein am letz - ten End die
den Leib in seim Schlaf - käm - mer - lein gar sanft ohn ein - ge

Tenor [Viola]
Ach Herr, lass dein lieb En - ge - lein am letz - ten End die
den Leib in seim Schlaf - käm - mer - lein gar sanft ohn ein - ge

Bass
Ach Herr, lass dein lieb En - ge - lein am letz - ten End die
den Leib in seim Schlaf - käm - mer - lein gar sanft ohn ein - ge

Continuo

S.
See - le mein in A - brahams Schoss tra - - gen,
Qual und Pein ruhn bis am jüng - sten Ta - - ge!

A.
See - le mein in A - bra - hams Schoss tra - - gen,
Qual und Pein ruhn bis am jüng - sten Ta - - ge!

T.
See - le mein in A - brahams Schoss tra - - gen,
Qual und Pein ruhn bis am jüng - sten Ta - - ge!

B.
See - le mein in A - bra - hams Schoss tra - - gen,
Qual und Pein ruhn bis am jüng - sten Ta - - ge!

B.C.

55. Salvator mundi

Edited by Dennis Shrock

John Blow

56. Remember not, Lord, our offences

Henry Purcell

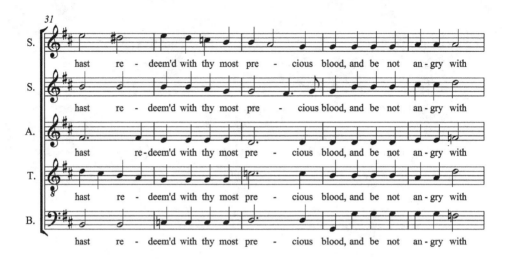

hast re - deem'd with thy most pre - cious blood, and be not an - gry with

us for - ev - er, be not an - gry with us for -

ev - - er, spare us, good Lord.

57. Saul
How excellent thy name, O Lord

Edited by Dennis Shrock

George Frideric Handel

58. Lord, let me know mine end

Edited by Dennis Shrock

Maurice Greene

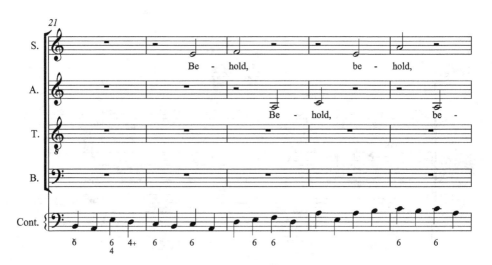

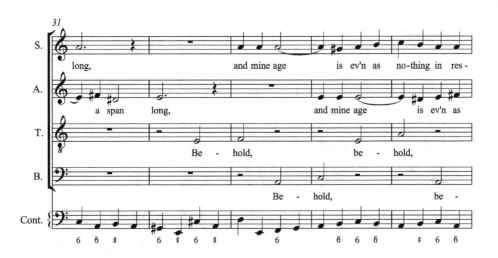

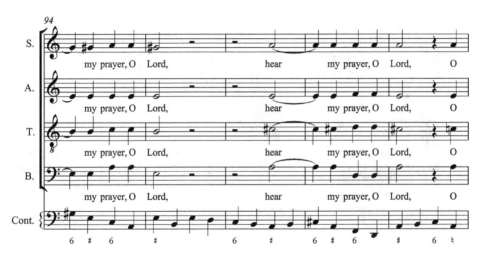

59. Versa est in luctum

Edited by Ng Tian Hui

Juan Gutiérrez de Padilla

60. Responsorio sequndo de SS José

Edited by Ng Tian Hui

Ignacio Jerusalem

The Classical Era

61. The Creation
Achieved is the glorious work

Edited by Bruce Mayhall Rastrelli

Joseph Haydn

62. Salve regina
MH634

Edited by Dennis Shrock

Michael Haydn

63. Requiem
Lacrimosa

Edited by Bruce Mayhall Rastrelli

Wolfgang Amadeus Mozart
completed by Süssmayr

64. Die Nacht

Franz Schubert

65. Requiem in C Minor
Graduale

Edited by Dennis Shrock

Luigi Cherubini

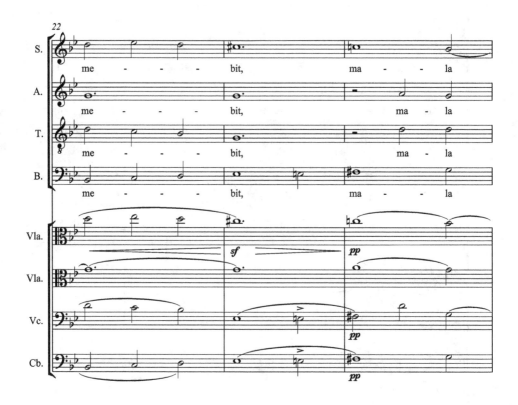

66. Stabat mater
Introduzione

Edited by Bruce Mayhall Rastrelli

Gioachino Rossini

67. Chester

William Billings

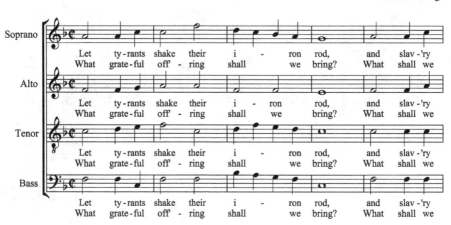

Let ty-rants shake their i - ron rod, and slav-'ry
What grate-ful off' - ring shall we bring? What shall we

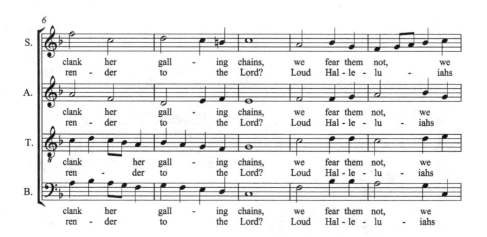

clank her gall - ing chains, we fear them not, we
ren - der to the Lord? Loud Hal - le - lu - iahs

trust in God, New Eng-land's God for ev - er reigns.
let us sing, and praise his name on ev' - ry chord.

THE ROMANTIC ERA

68. La damnation de Faust
Apothéose de Marguerite

Edited by Bruce Mayhall Rastrelli

Hector Berlioz

69. Calme des nuits

Camille Saint-Saëns

Molto Adagio

Soprano: Cal - me des nuits, frai - cheur des soirs,

Alto: Cal - me des nuits, frai - cheur des soirs,

Tenor: Cal - me des nuits, frai - cheur des soirs,

Bass: Cal - me des nuits, frai - cheur des soirs,

S.: vas - te scin - til - le - ment des mon - des,

A.: vas - te scin - til - le - ment des mon - des,

T.: vas - te scin - til - le - ment des mon - des,

B.: vas - te scin - til - le - ment des mon - des,

S.: grand si - len - ce des an - tres noirs vous char - mez les

A.: grand si - len - ce des an - tres noirs vous char - mez les

T.: grand si - len - ce des an - tres noirs vous char - mez les

B.: grand si - len - ce des an - tres noirs vous char - mez les

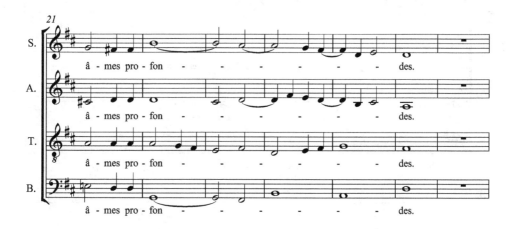

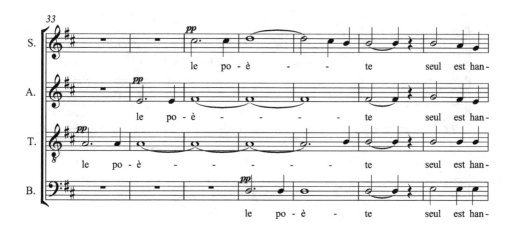

70. Requiem
Agnus Dei

Edited by Bruce Mayhall Rastrelli

Gabriel Fauré

71. Messa da Requiem
Sanctus

Edited by Bruce Mayhall Rastrelli

Giuseppe Verdi

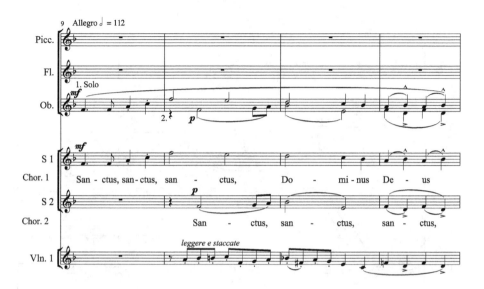

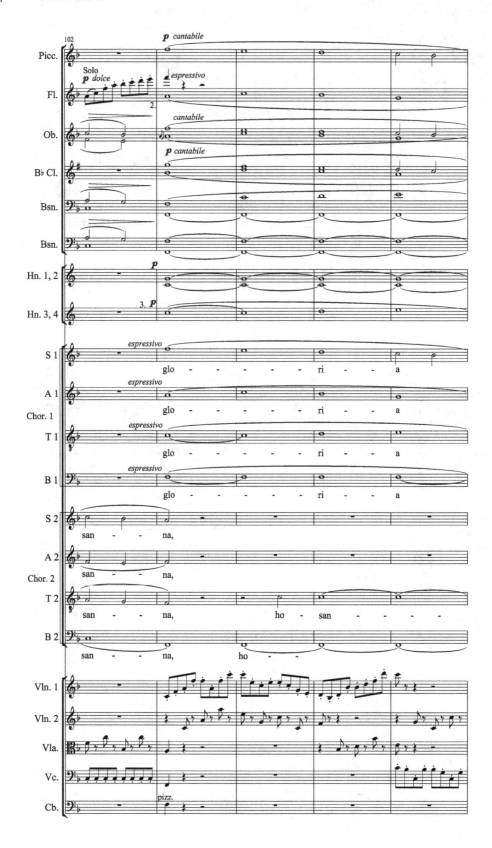

72. Missa in C Major
op.86
Kyrie

Edited by Bruce Mayhall Rastrelli

Ludwig van Beethoven

73. Elias / Elijah
Siehe, der Hüter Israels / He, watching over Israel

Edited by Bruce Mayhall Rastrelli   Felix Mendelssohn

74. Minnespiel
op.101
So wahr die Sonne scheinet

Robert Schumann

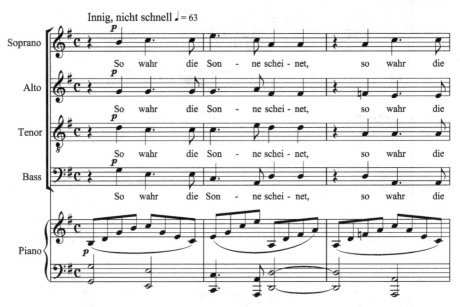

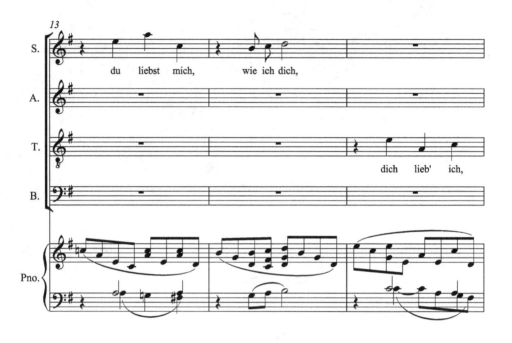

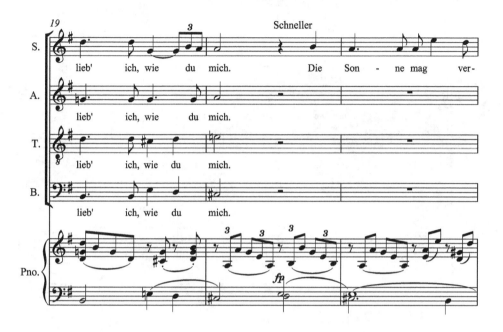

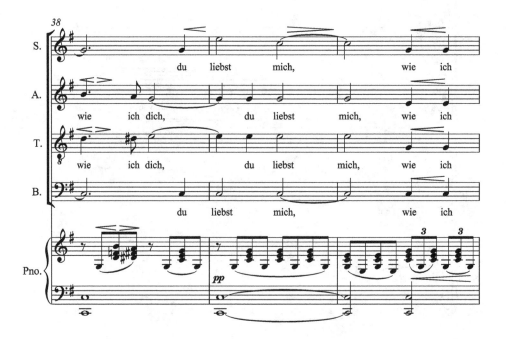

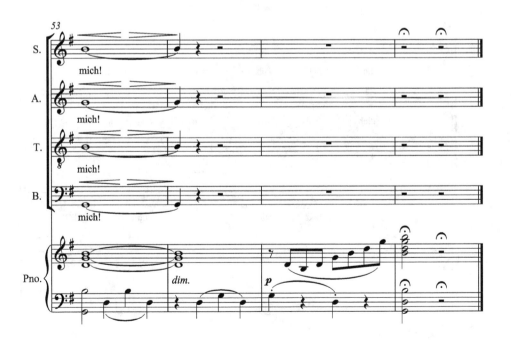

75. Ave verum

Franz Liszt

76. Os justi

Anton Bruckner

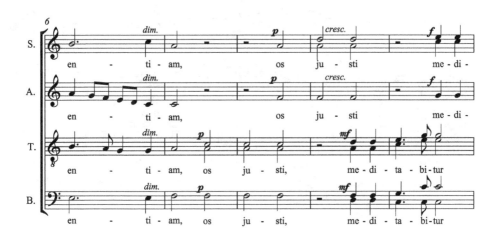

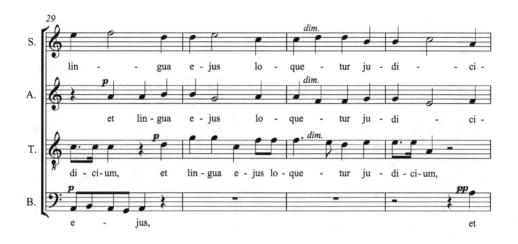

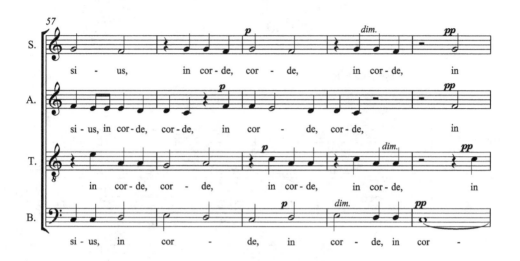

77. Ein deutsches Requiem
Selig sind, die da Leid tragen

Edited by Bruce Mayhall Rastrelli

Johannes Brahms

78. Waldesnacht, du wunderkühle

Johannes Brahms

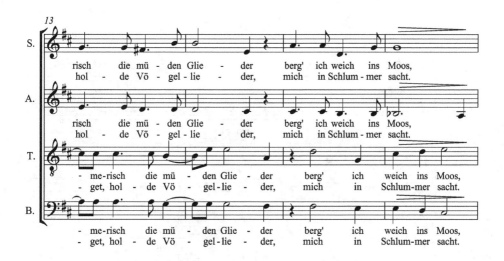

79. Abendlied

Joseph Rheinberger

80. V přírodě

Napadly písně v duši mou

Antonín Dvořák

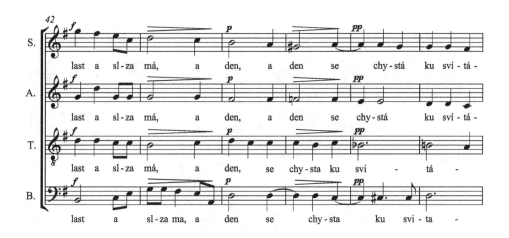

81. Otche nash

Anton Arensky

82. Svete tihiy

Aleksandr Grechaninov

83. Duh tvoy blagiy

Pavel Chesnokov

84. Vsenoshchnoye bdeniye

Bogoroditse devo

Serge Rachmaninoff

Bo - go - ro - dyi - tse Dye - vo, ra - - - duy -

sia, bla - go - dat - na - ya Ma - ri - - -

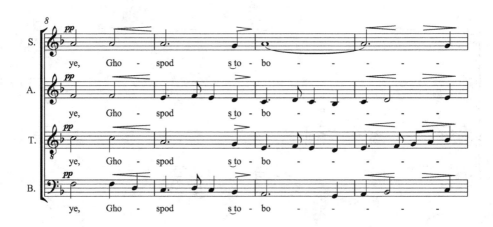

ye, Gho - spod s to - bo - - - - - -

85. Songs of Farewell
My soul, there is a country

Hubert Parry

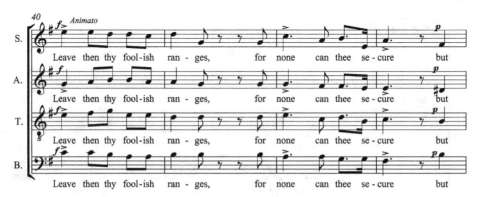

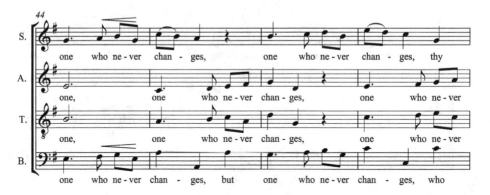

86. Beati quorum via

Charles Villiers Stanford

87. As torrents in summer

Edward Elgar

88. Nearer, my God, to thee

Lowell Mason

1. Near - er, my God, to thee, near - er to thee,
2. Tho' like the wan - der - er, the sun gone down,
3. There let the way ap - pear steps un - to heav'n,
4. Or if on joy - ful wing cleav - ing the sky,

e'en tho' it be a cross that rais - eth me;
dark - ness be ov - er me, my rest a stone;
all that thou send - est me in mer - cy giv'n;
sun, moon, and stars for - got, up - ward I fly;

still all my song shall be, near - er, my God, to thee,
yet in my dreams I'd be, near - er, my God, to thee,
an - gels to beck - on me, near - er, my God, to thee,
still all my song shall be, near - er, my God, to thee,

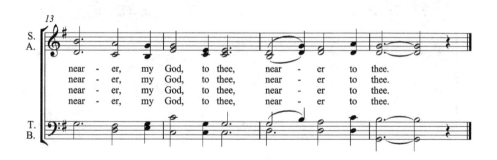

near - er, my God, to thee, near - er to thee.
near - er, my God, to thee, near - er to thee.
near - er, my God, to thee, near - er to thee.
near - er, my God, to thee, near - er to thee.

89. The brook

Edward MacDowell

90. Three Shakespeare Choruses
Through the house give glimmering light

Amy Beach

THE MODERN ERA

91. Trois Chansons de Charles d'Orléans
Dieu! qu'il la fait bon regarder

Claude Debussy

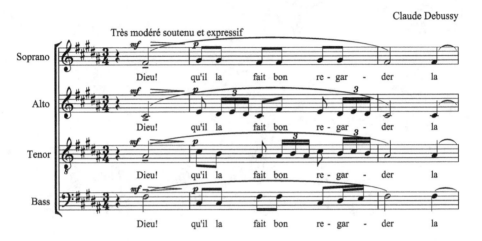

92. Trois Chansons
Nicolette

Maurice Ravel

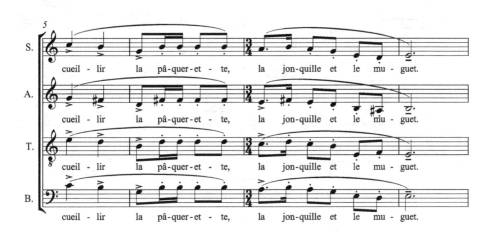

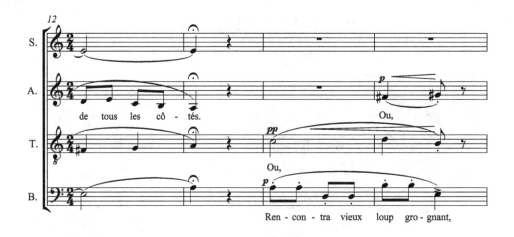

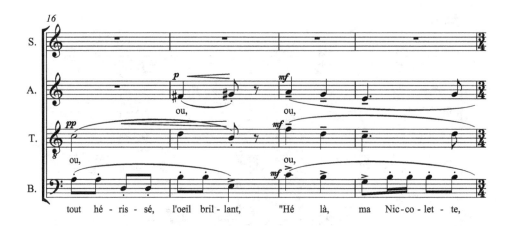

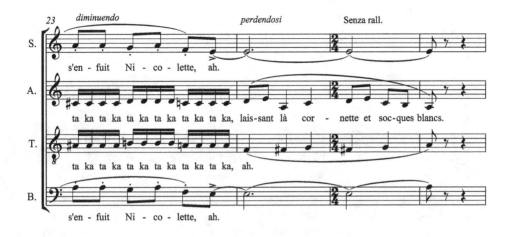

93. Mass
Agnus Dei

Frank Martin

94. Le roi David
La mort de David

Arthur Honegger

Le Récitant: L'esprit de Dieu parle pour moi. Un juste viendra sur les hommes, régnant dans la crainte de Dieu. C'est la clarté du matin, quand le soleil se lève. Oh! cette vie était si belle! Je te bénis, Toi qui me l'as donnée!

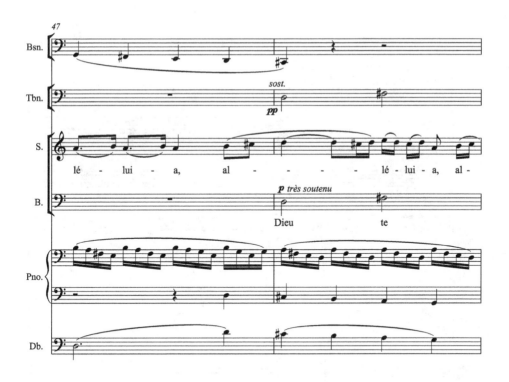

95. Vieille prière bouddhique
Prière quotidienne pour tout l'Univers

Edited by Bruce Mayhall Rastrelli

Lili Boulanger

96. Quatre motets pour le temps de Noël
Hodie Christus natus est

Francis Poulenc

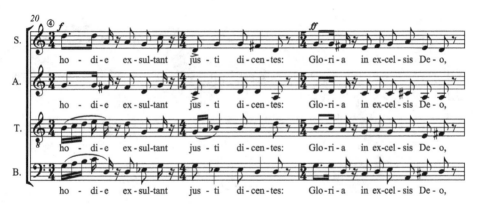

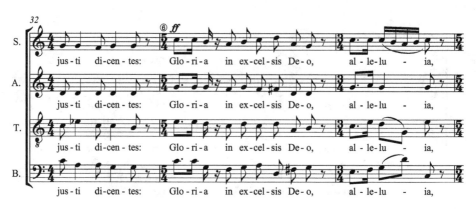

97. Requiem
In Paradisum

Maurice Duruflé

98. Vier Stücke
op. 27
Unentrinnbar

Arnold Schoenberg

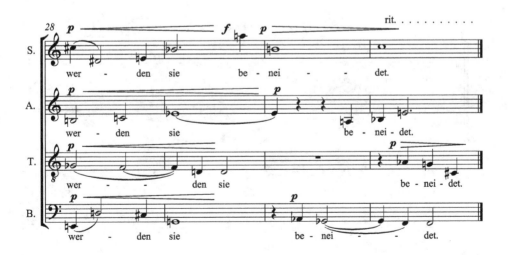

99. Entflieht auf leichten Kähnen

Anton Webern

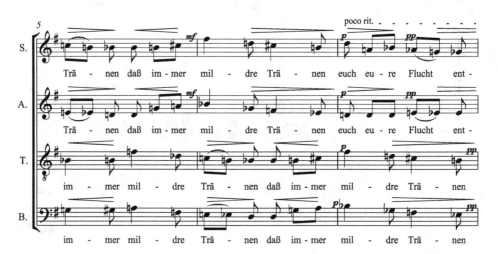

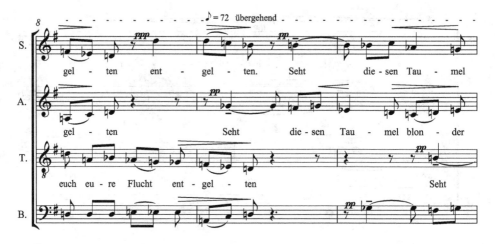

3

100. Six Chansons
La biche

Paul Hindemith

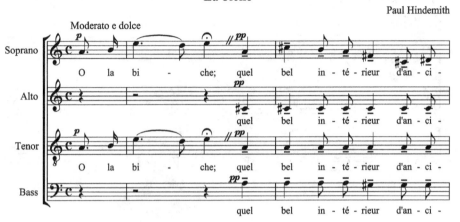

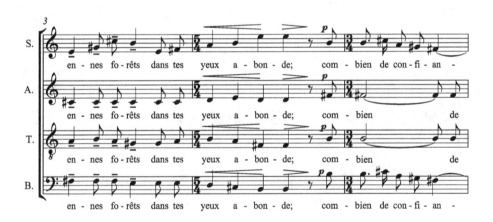

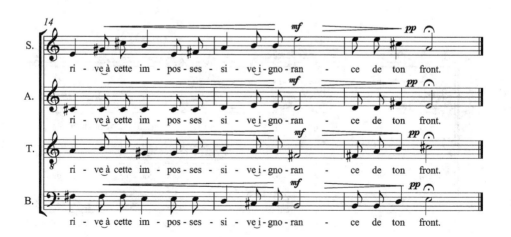

101. Lobe den Herren
op. 6/I, no. 2

Hugo Distler

102. O vos omnes

Pablo Casals

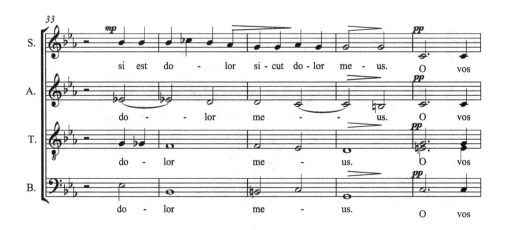

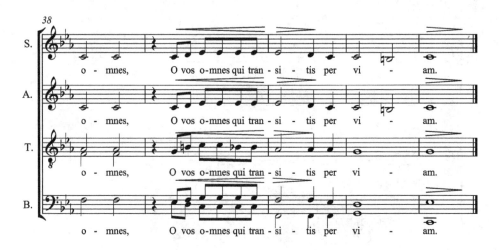

103. Sei cori di Michelangelo Buonarroti il giovane

Il coro delle malmaritate

Luigi Dallapiccola

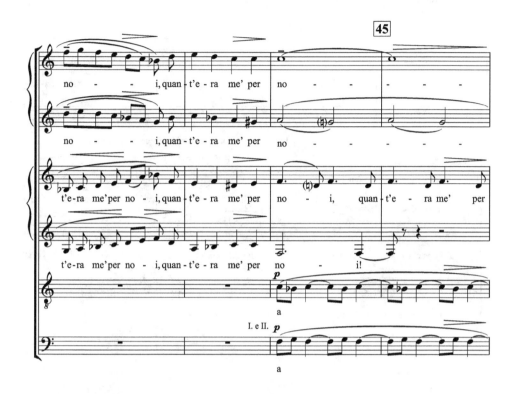

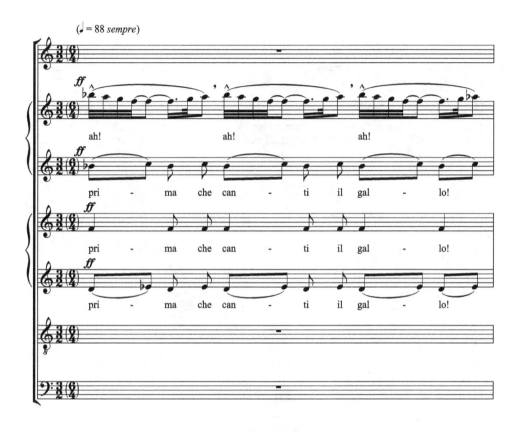

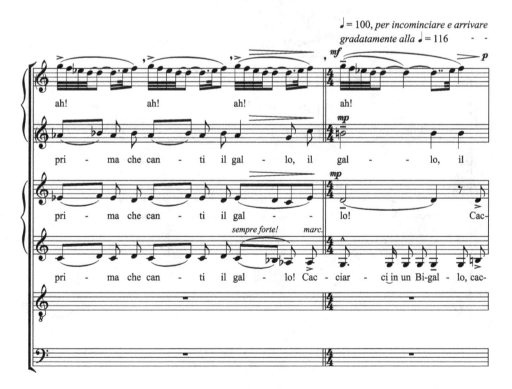

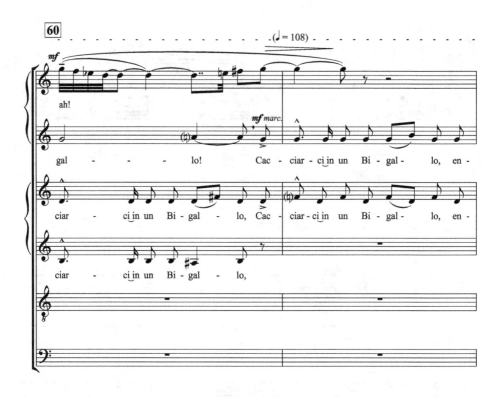

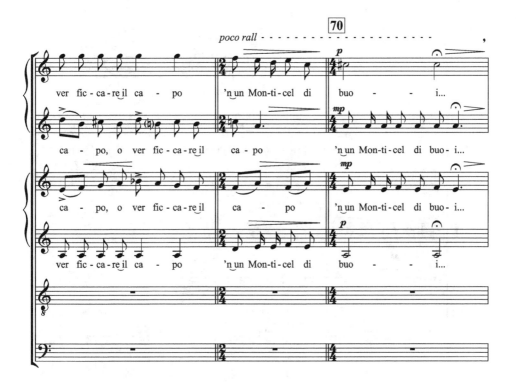

ben ben ben ben pri - - ma...

ben ben ben ben pri - ma... ch'e' non vi

ben ben ben ben pri - ma...

ben ben ben ben pri - ma...

ben ben ben ben pri - - ma...

ben ben ben ben pri - - ma...

li - ma, li - ma,

s'ab-bia a dir po-i: li - ma, li - ma. ch'e' non vi

Al-l'al trui spe-se, don-zel-le im-pa - ra - te...

Al-l'al trui spe-se, don-zel-le im-pa - ra - te...

li -

Al-l'al trui spe-se, don-zel-le im-pa - ra - te... li -

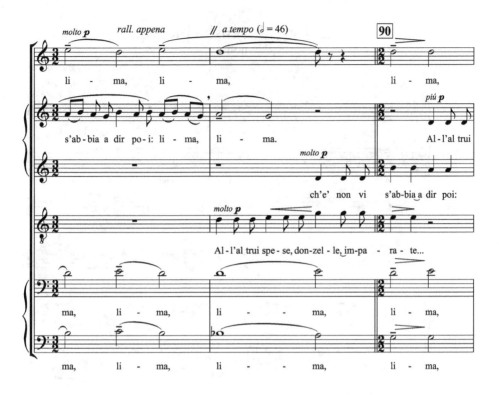

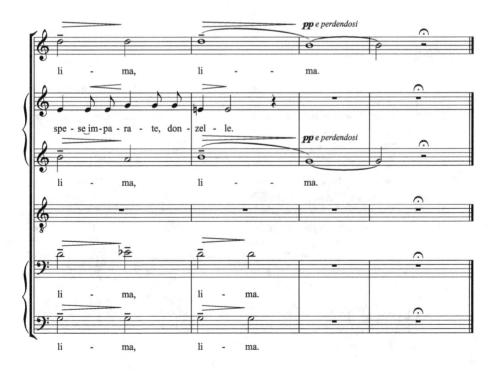

104. Štyri slovenské piesne

Na holi

Béla Bartók

105. Missa brevis
Kyrie

Zoltán Kodály

106. Passio et mors domini nostri Jesu Christi
secundum Lucam
(Final Scene)

Krzysztof Penderecki

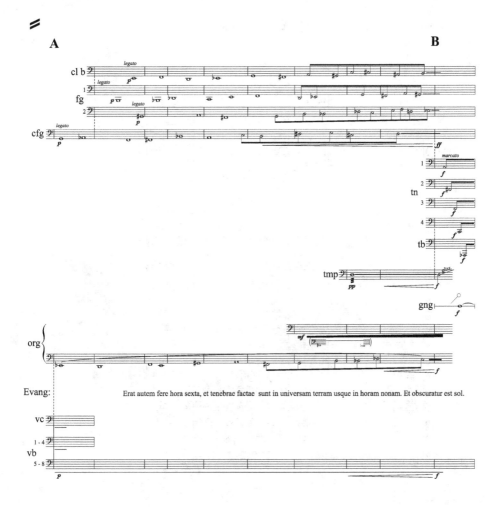

Erat autem fere hora sexta, et tenebrae factae sunt in universam terram usque in horam nonam. Et obscuratur est sol.

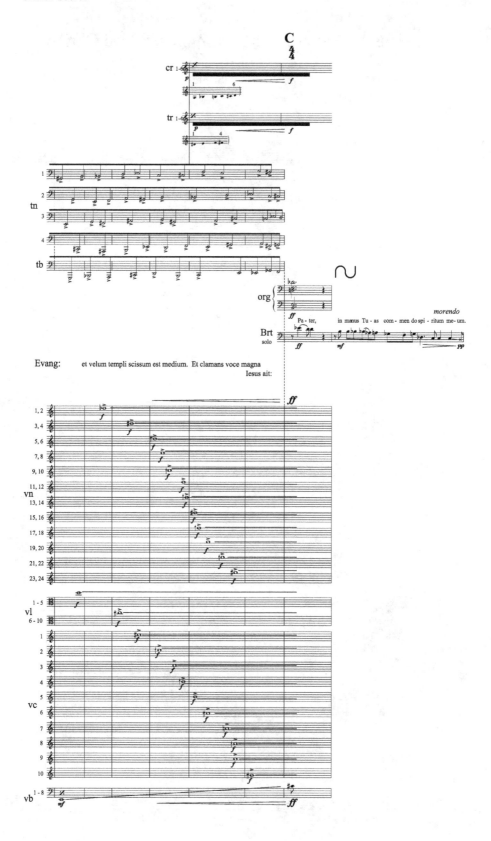

Pa - ter,   in manus Tu - as com - men do spi - ritum me - um.

morendo

Evang: et velum templi scissum est medium. Et clamans voce magna
                                        Iesus ait:

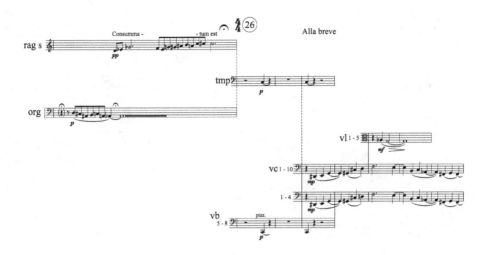

CORI

107. Mass
Gloria

Igor Stravinsky

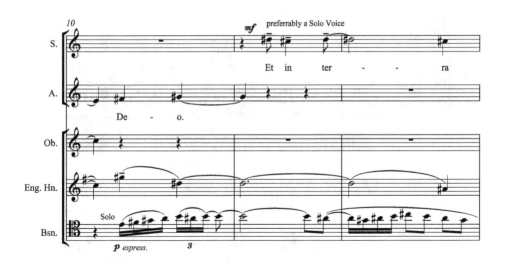

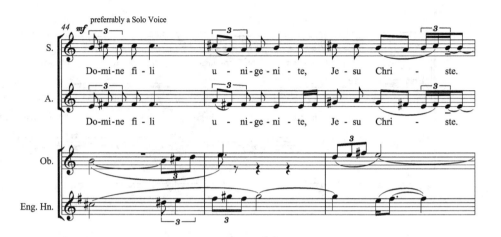

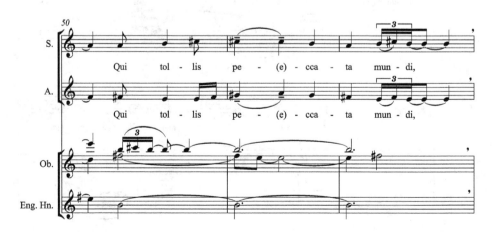

108. Aleksandr Nevsky
Aleksandr's Entry into Pskov

Edited by Bruce Mayhall Rastrelli

Sergey Prokofiev

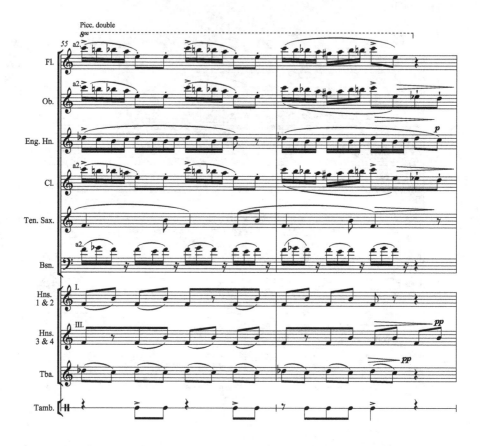

109. Laulusild

Veljo Tormis

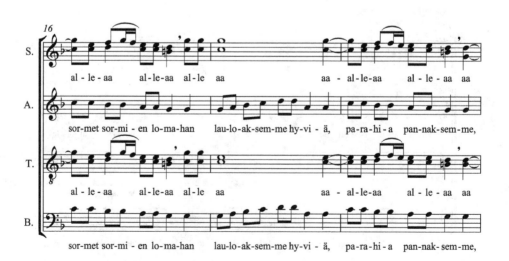

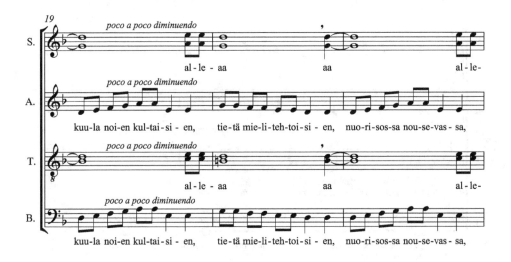

1. ma hak kan lau-le-mai e, al - le - aa,   al - le - aa, lau -
2. le - mai - e, las ke mai e, al - le - aa,   al - le - aa. aa

1. Lyö kä me kä - si kä - te - hen,   sor-met sor-mi-en lo - ma-han, Har-voin yh-te-hen y-hym-me,
2. lau-lo-ak sem-me hy-vi - ä,   pa - ra - hi - a pan-nak-sem-me.

aa

saam-me toi-nen toi - si-him - me   näil-la rau-koil-la ra-joil - la,   po-loi-sil - la Poh-jan mail - la.

uu

uu

110. Berliner Messe
Kyrie

Arvo Pärt

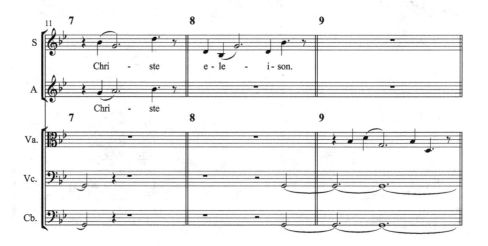

111. Finlandia

Jean Sibelius

112. Suite de Lorca
Canción de jinete

Einojuhani Rautavaara

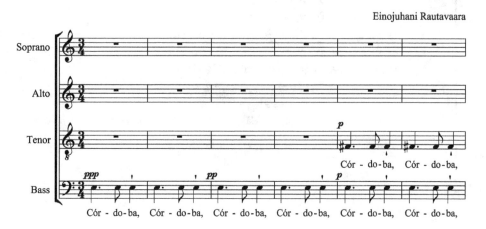

113. I hear the rain

Per Nørgård

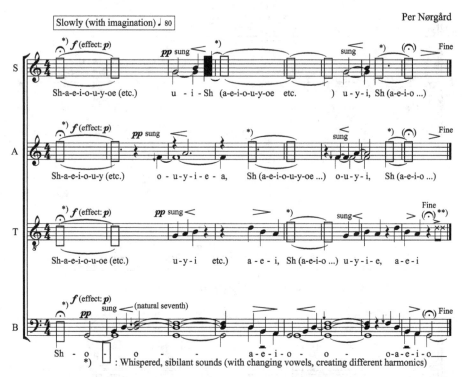

*) ⌐⌐ : Whispered, sibilant sounds (with changing vowels, creating different harmonics)

**) Fingersnaps and / or claves, small hand drum (at the edge) or the like. 2 or 3 of the tenors.

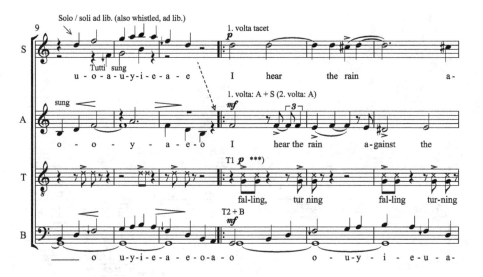

***) sung and fingersnapped / played

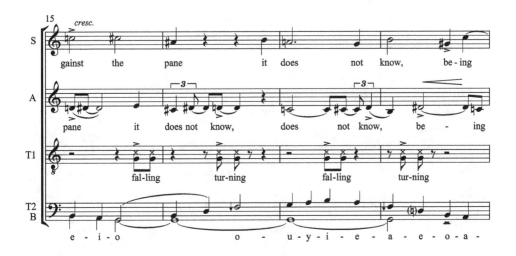

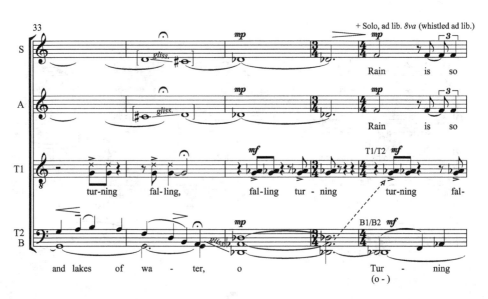

114. Five English Folk Songs
The dark-eyed sailor

Ralph Vaughan Williams

115. Lullay my liking

Gustav Holst

Lul - lay my lik - ing, my dear son, my sweet - ing,

lul - lay my dear heart, mine own dear darl - ing.

I saw a fair maid - en sit - ten and sing; she

lul - led a lit - tle child, a swee - te lord - ing.

That e - ter - nal lord is he that made al - le thing; of

al - le lord - es he is lord, of ev - 'ry king he's king.

There was mic - kle mel - o - dy at the child - es birth; though the

24

song - sters were hea - ven - ly they mad - e mic - kle mirth.

Refrain

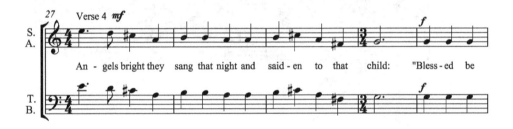

27 Verse 4 *mf*

An - gels bright they sang that night and said - en to that child: "Bless - ed be

32

thou and so be she that is so meek and mild."

Refrain

38 Verse 5 *p*

Pray we now to that child, as to his mo - ther dear, God

41

grant them all his bless - ing that now mak - en cheer.

Refrain

116. Like as the hart desireth the waterbrooks

Herbert Howells

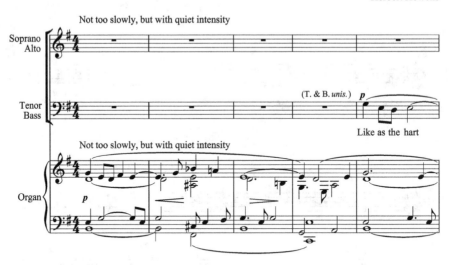

de - sir-eth the wa - ter - brooks,   so long-eth my soul af-ter thee,   O

God.   My soul   is   a - thirst   for

God,   yea, e - - ven for the liv - - ing God.

molto espressivo
When   shall I   come   to ap -
When   shall I   come
When   shall I   come   to ap -
When   shall I   come

dim. molto
pear   be-fore the   pre-sence   of   God?
to ap - pear   be-fore   God?
pear   be-fore the   pre-sence   of   God?
to ap - pear   be-fore   God?

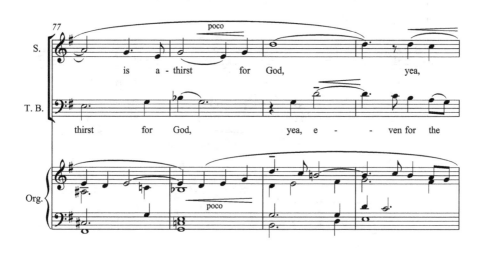

117. Set me as a seal upon thine heart

William Walton

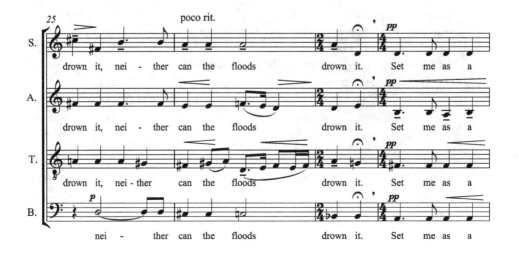

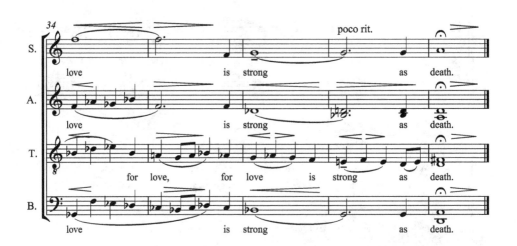

118. A Child of Our Time
Deep River

119. A Ceremony of Carols
Wolcum Yole

Benjamin Britten

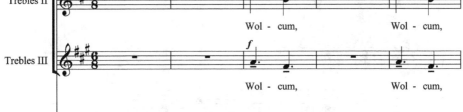

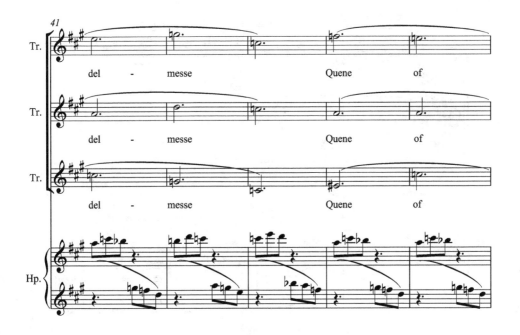

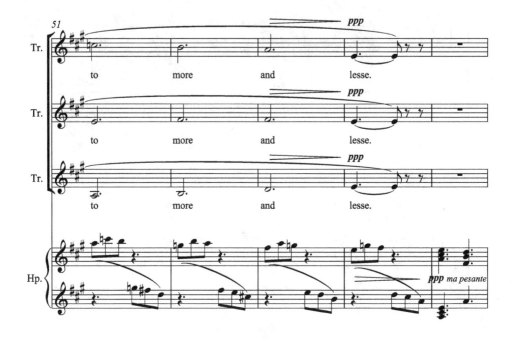

* *Piano glissando on white notes*

120. On the Underground
Set I - Benediction

Thea Musgrave

121. Hymn to the Mother of God

John Tavener

122. Three Harvest Home Chorales
Harvest Home #1

Charles Ives

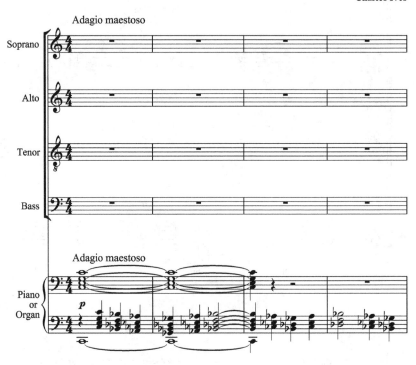

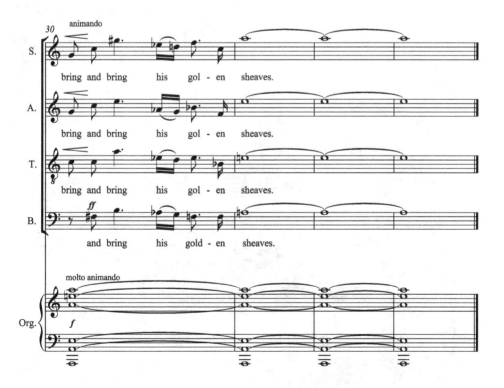

123. The Peaceable Kingdom
The paper reeds by the brooks

Randall Thompson

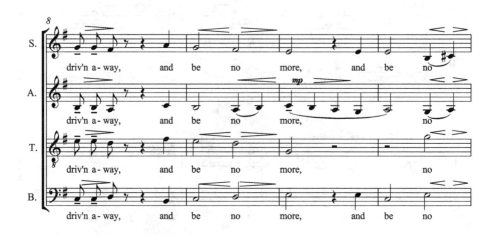

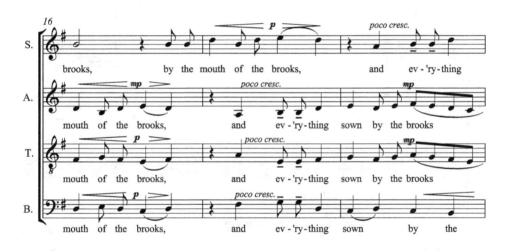

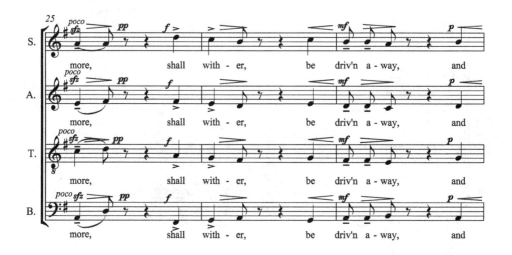

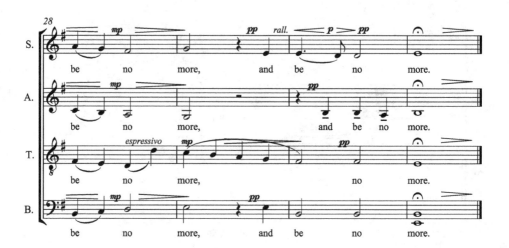

124. Flower Songs
Spouting Violets

Vincent Persichetti

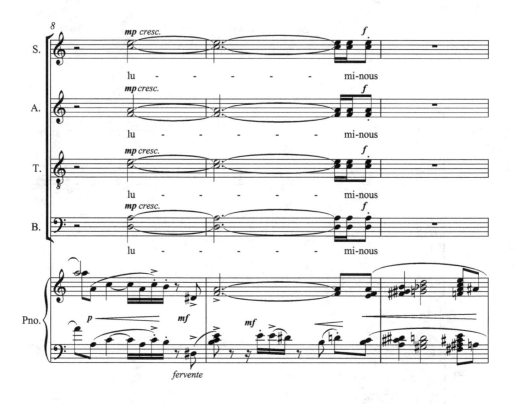

125. Four Elegies

At the round earth's imagin'd corners

Daniel Pinkham

sinnes a-bound, 'Tis late to aske a-bun-dance of thy grace, When wee are there; here on this

sinnes a-bound, When wee are there;

sinnes a-bound, 'Tis late to aske a-bun-dance of thy grace, When wee are there; here on this

sinnes a-bound,

low-ly ground. Teach mee how to re-pent; for that's as good As if thou had'st

Teach mee how to re-pent; for that's as good As if thou had'st

low-ly ground. for that's as good As if thou had'st

for that's as good As if thou had'st

For rehearsal only

seal'd my par-don,   with   thy   blood.

All whom the flood did, and fire shall o'er-

throw, All whom warre, dearth, age, a - gues,

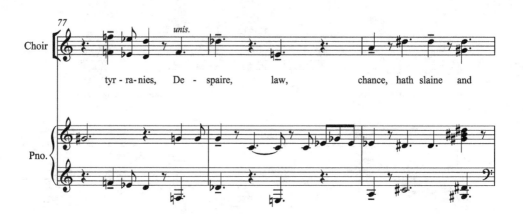

tyr - ra-nies, De - spaire, law, chance, hath slaine and

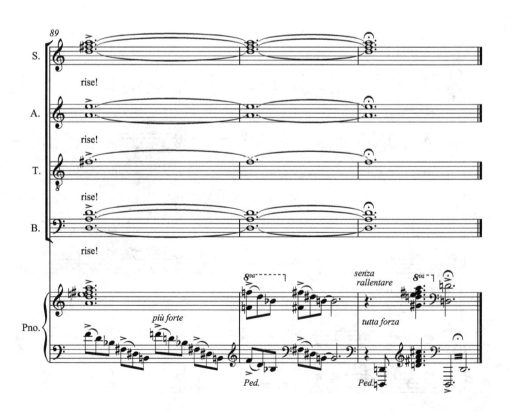

126. Four Madrigals
Love

Ned Rorem

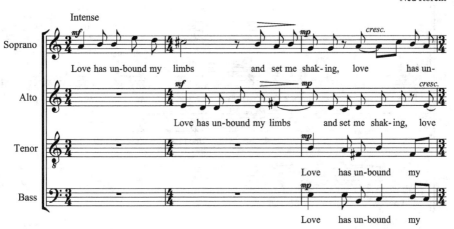

127. Peter Quince at the Clavier
Movement IV

Dominick Argento

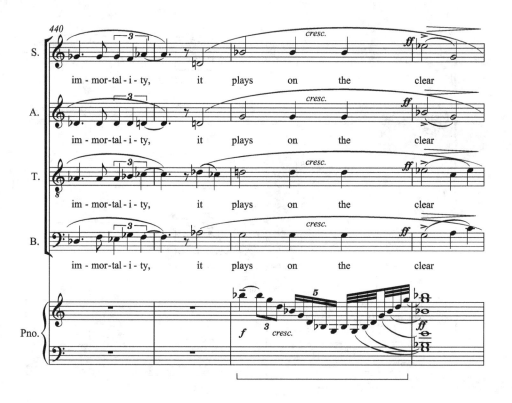

im - mor-tal - i - ty,   it   plays   on   the   clear

viol   of her mem - o - ry,

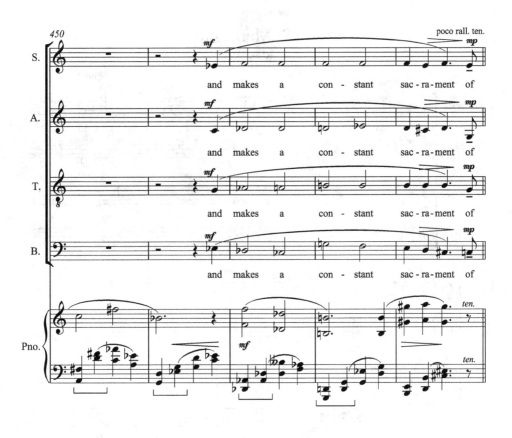

and makes a con-stant sac-ra-ment of

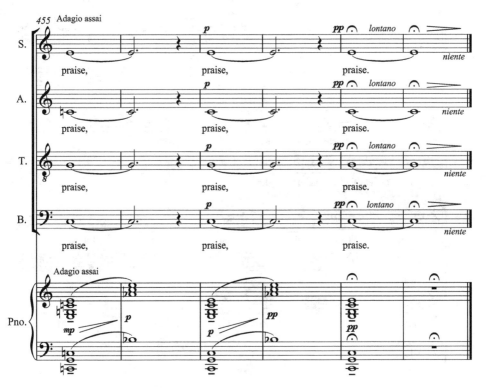

praise, praise, praise.

128. Madrigali
Amor, io sento l'alma

Morten Lauridsen

Lievemente, giocoso

129. Water Night

Eric Whitacre

NOTES AND TRANSLATIONS

1. ANONYMOUS—*SALVE REGINA*

This eleventh-century Gregorian chant is one of four so-called Marian antiphons (songs to the Virgin Mary) traditionally sung at the closing of the office of Compline or Vespers—*Salve regina* being sung from Trinity Sunday until the Saturday before the first Sunday of Advent. The musical style of the chant is neumatic in that text syllables set to single notes are combined with syllables set to short melismas. The musical structure contains several repetitive elements: the chant begins with two almost identical phrases; following those are two phrases that begin with similar musical motifs and textual phrases ("Ad te clamamus" and "Ad te suspiramus"); and the chant ends with three similar phrases. The beaming and sizing of notes in the transcription here attempt to emulate the shapes of the original Gregorian neumes, as well as to suggest the performance practice of semiology espoused at the Abbey of Solesmes. The text is believed to be by Hermann Contractus (1013–1054).

Hail, queen, merciful mother, life, sweetness, and our hope, hail. To you we cry, exiled, sons of Eve; to you we sigh, groaning and weeping in this valley of tears. Hasten, therefore, our advocate; turn to us those merciful eyes of yours; and Jesus, blessed fruit of your womb, show us after our exile, O merciful, O holy, O sweet Virgin Mary.

2. HILDEGARD VON BINGEN—*O VIRIDISSIMA VIRGA*

This is one of seventy-seven chants composed by Hildegard and contained in three volumes that together are entitled *Symphonia armonie celestium* (Symphony of the Harmony of Celestial Revelations). Hildegard most likely also composed the texts, many of which are about the Virgin Mary and St. Ursula and contain exotic imagery. The music is basically free in form, although many chants have repeated melodic patterns. In *O viridissima virga*, for instance, the rising pattern G–B–C–D appears nine times, and the similar rising pattern G–A–B–C appears seven times.

Oh greenest bloom, hail, which in the swift breeze proclaimed the calls of the saints. The time has now come that you flourish in your branches. Hail, hail to you, because the sun's heat perspires in you like the scent of balsam. Now in you blooms the beautiful flower, which gave scent to all those aromas that were once dried up. And all things were revealed in full freshness. Whence the skies gave dew upon the grass and all the land was made joyful, because her womb has produced fruit, and because the winged birds of the skies have made their nests in her.

3. Guillaume de Machaut—*Messe de nostre dame* (Kyrie)

Machaut's mass, which is the first-known cycle of the five portions of the Roman Catholic Ordinary, was likely composed in the 1360s for Saturday celebrations of the Lady Mass at Reims Cathedral. All of the movements except the Gloria and Credo are based on the Gregorian chant *Kyrie cunctipotens genitor* and are isometric in structure. In the Kyrie I, the tenor voice part is divided into seven talea (identical rhythmic patterns), while the contratenor (bass) part, with some inconsistencies, is in two talea. All four voice parts of the Christe are divided into three talea, and in addition, the rhythms of two of the parts are mirrored. Specifically: the triplum (soprano) and motetus (alto) each have talea that begin and end simultaneously; the tenor and contratenor are also paired with talea, although they do not line up with the triplum and mote-tus; and the tenor and contratenor rhythms, apart from the talea, are grouped in two-measure segments that mirror each other as seen from the beginning and end of the movement. The text is from the Ordinary of the Roman Catholic Mass.

Lord have mercy. Christ have mercy. Lord have mercy.

4. Johannes Ciconia—*Venecie, mundi splendor / Michael, qui Stena domus / Italie, mundicie*

Composed in 1405 to celebrate the Venetian victory in the war of expansion against the Carrara family, each of the motet's three voice parts has a different text that pays trib-ute to the city of Venice: the top part describes the splendor of the city; the middle part praises Michele Steno, doge of Venice from 1400 to 1413; and the bottom part is in the form of a short paean. Typical of polytextual motets from the Medieval era, the top two parts have fast-moving rhythmic textures that are related, while the lowest part is slower-moving and independent. Two typical characteristics of Ciconia's writing are seen at the end of the motet: passages of hocket and the incorporation of Ciconia's name. The text is by the composer.

Top voice part: *[O] Venice, the world's splendor, in Italy you are considered a beauty, in you exists all envy for standards of excellence. Rejoice, mother of the sea; salvation, cleansing every evil person; deter the waters, you are a marshland, you bearer of the unfortunate. Rejoice greatly, honorable maiden, you carry the miraculous works—to you alone are they entrusted—of a supreme lord. Rejoice, victress of foreigners, for the power of Venice yields not to the depraved, but conquers the earth and seas. For you bind the hands of the mighty, you restore peace within your portals, and you shatter the jaws of death for all your faithful. This is sung to you with a devout voice—and having been established, may Mary protect you—by Johannes Ciconia. [Amen.]*

Middle voice part: *[O] Michele, of the house of Stenos, your eminence who holds the dukedom, honor to you as a good man who leads a virtuous life. Like Phoebus, gentle prince, the world salutes you, "Hail"; palm who scatters fruit to your people, always our noble victor. Forgiving, commended as just, you are called a man of decency, you are the valued defender of the Catholic faith. You spread fitting gifts to the good, to the wicked you spread the sign of punishment in accordance with the laws and with the sword of justice. Wise, prudent, humble father—divine law being his mother—strong mind is your brother, you will be loved zealously by the republic. I pray that the seat be yours, servant of God in heaven, united at his throne forever and ever. [Amen.]*

Bottom voice part: *Italy, pure from all wickedness. Rejoice, mother of great merit. For you she sings with a devout voice. May Mary protect Johannes Ciconia.*

5. John Dunstable—Quam *pulcra es*

A motet in the discant or treble-dominated style of the late Medieval era, *Quam pulcra es* features Dunstable's distinctive tonal harmonic language, referred to as "contenance angloise" (English countenance). The mensuration signs (meter signatures) in the original manuscript indicate a perfect tempus and an imperfect prolation at the beginning of the piece (the measures divided into three beats and the beats divisible by two, resulting in 3/2 or 3/4) and an imperfect tempus and perfect prolation at measure 39 (the measures divided into two beats and the beats divisible by three, resulting in 6/4 or 6/8). Also, the fermata signs in measures 31 and 32 are original. The text is from the Song of Solomon 7:4–7, 11–12.

How beautiful and how lovely, my most beloved in delights. Your stature is like a palm tree, and your breasts like clusters of grapes. Your head is like Mount Carmel, your neck like a tower of ivory. Come, my love, let us go into the field, and see if the flowers give forth fruit, if the pomegranate blooms. There I will give my breasts to you. Alleluia.

6. Guillaume Dufay—*Missa L'homme armé* (Kyrie)

Dufay's *Missa L'homme armé* is perhaps the first of many masses during the Renaissance era to utilize the popular "L'homme armé" (The armed man) tune as a cantus firmus—the cantus firmus often being scored, as seen here, in long notes in the tenor voice part. The first third of the tune is in the tenor voice part of the first Kyrie, the middle of the tune is in the Christe, and the final third of the tune, which mirrors the beginning, is in the second Kyrie. Note that the beginning of the tune is stated in shorter rhythmic values at the end of the second Kyrie. The soprano and alto parts are constructed of free material, with occasional passages of imitation (e.g., measures 9 and 10). The bass part, typical of the early Renaissance, is in slower-moving rhythmic values. The text is from the Ordinary of the Roman Catholic Mass. See #3.

7. Josquin Desprez—*Missa de beata virgine* (Agnus Dei)

The *Missa de beata virgine* (Mass of the blessed virgin), Josquin's most popular mass during the Renaissance era, uses a different Marian chant as the structural basis for each movement. In the opening and closing portions of the Agnus Dei, the chant is paraphrased in the second tenor voice part and then treated in strict canon in the alto part. The middle of the movement (traditionally the repeat of the first line of text) is a duet, generally referred to as a *bicinium*. The text is from the Ordinary of the Roman Catholic Mass.

Lamb of God, who takes away the sins of the world, have mercy on us. Lamb of God, who takes away the sins of the world, have mercy on us. Lamb of God, who takes away the sins of the world, grant us peace.

8. Clément Janequin—*Au joli jeu*

This is an example of the Parisian chanson, a relatively homophonic version of the Renaissance chanson made popular during the middle and late years of the sixteenth century through printings by such publishers as Pierre Attaingnant. The textures of the Parisian chansons consist of alternating passages of simple imitation and homophony, with occasional duet exchanges and repeated rhythmic patterns. The texts are often of a lighthearted or humorous nature and frequently deal with courtship and amorous adventures.

The jolly game of pushing is good to play. The other day I was going about my way when I met a beauty with a nice body. Smiling sweetly, I went to kiss her; she doubted my intentions, but I pressed on. Let it happen; I didn't want to accept a refusal. I spoke to her lovingly; she snickered, danced without music, and let it happen.

9. Claude Goudimel—*Ainsi qu'on oit le cerf bruire*

Printed here are two settings of Psalm 42 composed by Goudimel for the Calvinist Church. The first setting, with text to verse 1 of the psalm, is in a simple hymn-like style; the melody—from the *Geneva Psalter* and called "Geneva 42" today—is in the tenor voice part. The second setting, to verse 2, is in a slightly elaborated style, with the melody in the soprano voice part and with the other voice parts polyphonically independent. See the commentary to #11 for more detailed information about Calvinist psalm settings.

1. *As one hears the cry of the deer longing for the fresh waters of the brook, so longs my heart as it sighs, my God, after your brook. It is always crying, yearning, for the great, the great God alive. Alas, when will be the time that I see the face of God?*

2. *Day and night for my body I cry and search for sustenance, and while I search I am asked, where is your God now? I become weak as I remember that I used to lead gatherings, praying, singing, with the multitudes, to take to the temple an offering.*

10. CLAUDE LE JEUNE—*AMOUR CRUEL QUE PENSE TU*

This chanson, like Le Jeune's more famous *Revoici venir du printemps*, is an example of the *vers mesurée* or *musique mesurée* style of composition popular for a brief period of time in France during the late sixteenth century. The style, which adhered to the precepts of the Académie de Poésie et de Musique formed by Jean-Antoine Baïf, is characterized by long and short note values set to corresponding accented and unaccented text syllables, thus resulting in a metrically free but patterned rhythmic texture. The style is also characterized by a structure of verses (called *chants*) and a refrain (called a *rechant*) that are varied in voicings.

1. *Cruel love, what are you thinking, pulling away with so much harshness? I have neither soul nor heart to take advantage of your virtue. You know very well that you have me imprisoned, and I am held with strong bonds of cruelty that you use, the queen of beauty.*
2. *Alas, you are blind not to know this. Find another target other than me, one who will weaken under you. Turn your bow away from me and from now on aim it elsewhere, towards a higher goal and thus claim a greater glory.*
3. *Go and strike this beauty, this pride. Break this zeal, break this hard heart, the heart that disdains your grandeur. There, show what your strikes can do to all, and you will make yourself softened to my cries for pity and my afflictions.*

11. JAN PIETERSZOON SWEELINCK—*OR SUS, SERVITEURS DU SEIGNEUR*

Settings of psalm texts in French from the late Renaissance are comparable in styles and purposes to settings of Lutheran chorales in German. The French pieces were used in worship services and private devotionals by the Huguenots (members of the Protestant Reformed Church of France or the French Calvinists) and were mainly based on tunes in the Genevan Psalter. Like German Lutheran chorale settings, the French psalm settings were composed in three styles: hymn-like, with the tune in the tenor voice part; slightly adorned, with the tune in the soprano voice part and imitative phrases in the other parts; and motet-like, with imitative phrases in all parts. Sweelink's setting here, which is based on the tune generally referred to as "Old Hundredth," is basically in the second style, although the tune is not restricted to the soprano voice part; it appears first in the bass, then in the soprano, and finally in the tenor. The text is from Psalm 134:1.

Let us now, servants of the Lord, who by night in his honor, stand in his house in service, give praise and elevate his name. Lift your hands on high and to the holy temple of God, and to him who is worthy, recite your prayers aloud. God, who has made and framed the earth and sky by his power, from Mount Sion on high, his good face made appearance.

12. PHILIPPE VERDELOT—*ITALIA MIA*

The Italian madrigal was generally a serious secular art form at the beginning of the Renaissance era, with texts by famed poets that address weighty subjects and with music in the learned style of motets. The text of *Italia mia* comes from the first paragraph of a letter written by Francesco Petrarca (1304–1374), one of the greatest poets in Italian history. Petrarch's letter, although referring to the many wars that raged in Italy during the fourteenth century, was probably written in response to the war between Parma and Milan in the 1340s. Verdelot's madrigal, considered one of the finest examples of the genre, alternates passages of homophony with imitative polyphony and treats the poetry in a narrative fashion, with very little text repetition. Verdelot further aids in the expression of the text by shaping harmonic tension to reflect natural spoken declamation and to coincide with cadential pauses.

My Italy, though words are no remedy for the many mortal wounds that I see in your beautiful body, I would like at least my sighs to be such as hopes for the Tiber and Arno and Po, where sorrowful and sad I now sit. Ruler of heaven, I ask that the pity that led you to earth may turn you toward your beloved divine country. See, noble lord, from what trivial causes arises such a cruel war; and the hearts, hardened and closed by Mars proud and fierce, do you open, father, and soften and free. There make your truth, however unworthy I may be, through my tongue be heard.

13. JACQUES ARCADELT—*IO DICO CHE FRA VOI*

Like Verdelot's *Italia mia*, this is an example of the Italian madrigal in the early part of the Renaissance era. Arcadelt's textures are basically homophonic, with brief portions of free imitation (e.g., the phrase "poi che sarete morti" in measures 10–12); the harmonic language is tonal, with regular cadences in the tonic key at the ends of major text phrases; and the final phrase of the madrigal is repeated (measures 37–41 are nearly identical to measures 42–46). The text is by the renowned sculptor and painter Michelangelo Buonarroti (1475–1564).

I say that among you, powerful gods, every adversity should be borne patiently, and when you are dead, through a thousand wrongs and injuries, and she loves you as you now burn for her, you can justly take revenge for them. Alas, wretched is he who unhappily waits, and goes on waiting for me to finally bring him comfort. And yet you should know well, that a generous, proud, and noble heart, pardons and bears love toward the one who hurts him.

14. CIPRIANO DE RORE—*ANCOR CHE COL PARTIRE*

Rore was one of the chief composers of the Italian madrigal during its second period of development in the Renaissance era. As seen in *Ancor che col partire*, the texts are often about unrequited
love and are written by contemporary poets of minor status (unlike poets such as Petrarch and
Michelangelo, whose works were used in the early Italian madrigal). The music consists of short
rhythmic values that are referred to as *note nere* (black notes), concise phrases of music, and
varied imitative textures that include duet passages. The text is by Alfonso d'Avalos (1502–1546).

*Although in parting I feel I am dying, I would part every hour, every moment, so great is the pleasure
I feel in the life I gain on my return. And so thousands and thousands of times a day I would part
from you, so sweet are my returns.*

15. GIOVANNI PIERLUIGI DA PALESTRINA—*TU ES PETRUS – QUODCUMQUE LIGAVERIS*

Palestrina's motet is an example of the multisectional construction prevalent in madrigals
and motets during the middle and late years of the Renaissance era: the music is divided
into distinct and separate parts or movements. In *Tu es Petrus – Quodcumque ligaveris*, the
prima pars (first part) and *secunda pars* (second part) each end with the same text and music.
Palestrina's writing is also an example of pervasive imitation: each phrase of text and music
is imitated throughout all the voice parts. Furthermore, the motet has aspects of the dialogue style, seen between the upper and lower voices at the beginning of the motet's two
parts and between the soprano and bass voices thereafter (the first soprano and the bass
dialogue with the second soprano and baritone). It is interesting to note that Palestrina
increases the number of voices that sound simultaneously as the major phrases cadence,
and that the only instances of all voices scored together homophonically are at two statements of the word "claves" (keys) near the end of each part of the motet. The text is from
Matthew 16:18–19.

*You are Peter, and upon this rock I will build my church, and the gates of hell will not prevail against
it, and I will give you the keys to the kingdom of heaven. Whatsoever is bound on earth will be bound
also in heaven, and whatsoever will be free on earth will be free also in heaven, and I will give you the
keys to the kingdom of heaven.*

16. GIOVANNI PIERLUIGI DA PALESTRINA—*MISSA TU ES PETRUS* (KYRIE)

Palestrina's mass is an example of the parody technique, which was employed frequently
during the Renaissance era. The musical material of the mass is derived from a preexisting

composition—in this case, Palestrina's motet of the same name. The opening two measures of the Kyrie are almost identical to the opening of the motet, although the upper and lower voices are interchanged and further statements of the "Kyrie eleison" text come from phrases within the motet's first point of imitation (e.g., the first soprano part of measures 12–15 in the mass is from measures 3–6 of the second soprano part in the motet, and measures 15–18 of the bass part in the mass, as well as most of the phrases in the latter half of the first Kyrie, are drawn from measures 9–12 of the bass part in the motet). The phrases in the Christe are drawn from measures 15–18 (the "aedificabo ecclesiam meam" text) of the bass part in the motet, and the music at the beginning of the second Kyrie comes from measures 32–35 of the first soprano part in the motet (the "et portae inferi" text). The end of the second Kyrie is based on the "claves regni" material of the motet. The entire Kyrie of the mass is, therefore, built on music from the entire first part of the motet. The text is from the Ordinary of the Roman Catholic Mass. See #3.

17. Orazio Vecchi—*Fa una canzona*

Vecchi, who was famous for his madrigal comedy *L'Amfiparnaso*, composed six books of canzonets—the canzonet being a popular secular genre during the latter part of the Renaissance era that, with a homophonic texture, song-like melody in the top voice part, and humorous or lighthearted text, served as a counterpart to the serious musical and textual nature of the Italian madrigal. *Fa una canzona* pokes fun at the *note nere* (black note) style of composition, which was characterized by dense rhythmic textures of quarter, eighth, and sixteenth notes and often contained sharp harmonic dissonances and complex mensuration formulas. The text is strophic, with five verses (only three of which are shown in the score) and a refrain common to each verse.

1. *Make a canzonet without black notes, if you ever have wanted my favor; make it in a mode that invites sleep, sweetly making it come to an end.*
2. *Don't put in harsh dissonances, because my ears are not accustomed to them. . . .*
3. *Don't put in proportions or complex signs, over everything this is my design. . . .*
4. *And then you will have a style that Orfeo used to placate Prosperina in the depths. . . .*
5. *The same style that sweetly quieted the evil spirit in Saul. . . .*

18. Luca Marenzio—*Leggiadre ninfe*

This is one of twenty-nine madrigals contained in *Il trionfo di Dori*, a collection of Italian madrigals composed by the most famous madrigalists of the time and published in Venice in 1592. All the madrigals in the collection are for six voice parts, with textures that alternate between homophony and simple imitative polyphony, and all the madrigals end with the text "Viva la bella Dori" (Long live fair Dori). The exact derivation of this phrase is unknown, although it is believed to be a reference to the bride of Leonardo Sanudo, a Venetian nobleman who commissioned all the poems for *Il trionfo di Dori*. The publisher of the music, Angelo Gardano, also dedicated the madrigals to Sanudo. The collection was the model for the similar English publication entitled *The Triumphs of Oriana*, published in 1601.

Graceful nymphs and loving shepherds, with what happy countenance, in this shady valley by the clear ripples of this lively fountain, today you were drawn by Love to choose flower by flower to weave little garlands and crowns for my gentle nymph. While charming satyrs and sylvans in their exotic dress dance with modest humility, you sing, scattering roses and flowers, "Long live fair Dori."

19. GIOVANNI GIACOMO GASTOLDI—*AMOR VITTORIOSO*

This is an example of the balletto, which, like the canzonet, was a popular counterpart to the Italian madrigal during the Renaissance era. While the madrigal employed serious texts and was generally imitative in texture, the balletto was characterized by homophonic textures, dance-like rhythms, lighthearted subject matter, sections of "fa la la" text at the ends of major poetic lines, and strophic structures. The title of the balletto translates as "Victorious Love." The text is by the composer. All four of the original verses are printed here, although only the first two verses are shown in the score.

1. *Everyone come armed, O my strong soldiers, fa la la.*
   I am unconquered Love, the skillful archer.
   Fear not at all, but in fine ranks united follow me courageously, fa la la.
2. *They seem to be great heroes, those who are against you, fa la la.*
   But those who might hurt you, they cannot defend themselves.
   Fear not at all, but courageously and strong be lively and fight, fa la la.
3. *Happily now move your feet, let yours be the prizes, fa la la.*
   Now let us beat scorn away, for it does not deserve to live.
   Fear not at all, the glory will be eternal and victory is assured, fa la la.
4. *He already lies dead on the ground, he who had fought against us, fa la la.*
   Now we will boldly crush all his other followers.
   Fear not at all, look at those who are not dead run away, scattered and defeated, fa la la.

20. GIOVANNI GABRIELI—*HODIE CHRISTUS NATUS EST*

Gabrieli's motet represents the "cori spezzati" (divided or broken choirs) style of composition that was popular at St. Mark's Basilica in Venice during the latter years of the Renaissance era. Typical of this style, which is also referred to as "polychoral," are phrases of dialogue between the choirs, alternating passages of homophony and simple imitative polyphony, and sections of triple meter interspersed within the predominately duple texture. The text is from Luke 2:11 and 13–14.

Today Christ is born, today the savior has appeared; today on earth the angels sing, the archangels rejoice; today the righteous exult, saying: Glory to God in the highest, and on earth peace to men of goodwill.

21. Carlo Gesualdo—*Resta di darmi noia*

Gesualdo is known for the madrigals composed late in his life that exhibit abrupt changes in texture, idiosyncratic chromaticism, and unexpected harmonic shifts. These traits, often referred to as "mannered" in style, are evident in *Resta di darmi noia*, from his sixth and final book of madrigals, published in 1611. In addition, each verbal image of text is treated separately and often set off by rests (e.g., measures 1, 4, and 13–14), and the second half of the madrigal is repeated.

Cease troubling me, thought cruel and vain, for it can never be that which pleases you!
Death is for me a joy, hope is not permitted, or to be happier.

22. Cristóbal de Morales—*Magnificat primi toni* (Anima mea)

Morales composed two cycles of the Magnificat text, each cycle consisting of settings on the eight Gregorian chant tones and each setting titled according to those tones (*primi toni, secundi toni, tertii toni*, etc.). Typical of the time, each setting was also composed in alternatim style (sections of polyphony alternating with sections of chant) and subtitled according to the verse of text that begins the polyphony ("Anima mea" being the first verse of the Magnificat text). Also typical, the verses have varied scorings. In the setting here by Morales, which was popular throughout Europe, the repetitive chant tone is incorporated into the soprano voice part (e.g., "Quia respexit humilitatem ancillae suae"), and the other parts are coordinated through independent imitative phrases. The following translation is only of every other verse—the verses of text set by Morales.

My soul [magnifies] the Lord. For he has regarded the low estate of his handmaiden: for behold, henceforth all generations will call me blessed. And his mercy is on them who fear him from generation to generation. He has deposed the mighty from their seats, and exalted the humble. He has helped his servant Israel, in remembrance of his mercy. Glory to the father and son and holy spirit.

23. Francisco Guerrero—*A un niño llorando*

This is an example of a villancico—a popular genre in Spain and the New World during the latter part of the Renaissance era, often set to Christmas texts and structured of verses or stanzas, called *coplas* (numbers 2 and 4 below), and a refrain, called an *estribillo* (numbers 1, 3, and 5 below). The verses are generally soloistic in nature (often scored for a single voice a cappella), while the refrains are mainly choral.

1. *To a young child crying in the cold go three kings to adore, because the child can give kingdom, life, glory, and heaven.*
2. *He is born with such lowliness, although he is a powerful king, because he is lawfully giving us humbleness and poverty.*
3. *To him crying in the cold, three kings go to adore him. . . .*
4. *Come, also my soul, to adore such a high name, and you will see that this child is man and the firstborn son of God.*
5. *And although he is poor and very small, the kings go to adore him. . . .*

24. Tomás Luis de Victoria—*Vere languores nostros*

Victoria's *Vere languores nostros*, along with his other famous motets *O magnum mysterium* and *Ave Maria*, represent writing in the late Renaissance that was economical in scoring, uncluttered in texture, balanced in length and distribution of phrases, and expressive in harmonic construction and text setting. In particular, the textures consist of homophonic sections that alternate with short passages of uncomplicated polyphony, the text is mainly syllabic in its rhythmic setting, and the phrases, separated by rests, impart a sense of natural declamation. The text is from Isaiah 53:4–5 and the Tenebrae services for Maundy Thursday.

Truly our weaknesses he alone has borne, and our sorrows he himself has carried; through his stripes we were healed. Sweet wood, sweet nails, sweet heavy tree, which alone was found worthy to bear the king and Lord of heaven.

25. Heinrich Isaac—*Innsbruck, ich muss dich lassen*

Composed in 1539, this is the most famous lied (song) of the Renaissance era. Typical of the genre, it has a German secular text, homophonic texture, strophic structure, and prominent melody in the soprano voice part. It also has a repeat design, which gives the piece an AABB form. While Isaac most certainly composed the alto, tenor, and bass voice parts, the soprano melody may have been a preexisting folk song. After Isaac's setting, the melody became famous as a contrafactum, with the sacred text "O Welt, ich muss dich lassen" (O world, I must leave you) used frequently as a chorale by German Baroque composers. Only one of the three verses is shown in the score.

1. *Innsbruck, I must leave you, I go on my way, to a foreign land; my joy is taken from me, which I know not how to regain, since I am suffering so.*
2. *I must now bear a great sorrow, which I alone can lament, to my dearest loved one; ah dear, let the poor man that I am, feel in my heart your pity, that I must go away.*
3. *You comfort me above all women, I will be yours forever, staying true, your honor preserving; now God must protect you, in all virtue keeping you, until I return.*

26. ORLANDO DI LASSO—*MUSICA DEI DONUM OPTIMI*

This is one of a limited number of Renaissance motets composed to a secular text (one that was also set by several other composers, including Lasso's contemporary, Jacobus Vaet). Lasso divided the three phrases of text into three extended points of imitation, isolating the word "musica" as its own short point and writing near-identical music to each of its statements. This compositional procedure gives the motet an ABACAD-like form. However, because Lasso also repeats most of the second half of the D section (that portion of the phrase set to the text "et horridas movet ferras"), the form is in reality ABACADD.

Music, God's greatest gift, draws forth men, draws forth God. Music calms fierce souls, gladdens sad minds. Music even moves trees and horrible beasts.

27. ORLANDO DI LASSO—*TUTTO LO DÌ*

Lasso composed in all the genres of his day—from serious and learned motets, masses, and madrigals to lighthearted and proletarian villanellas, morescas, and canzonets. As a villanella, *Tutto lo dì* is mainly homophonic in texture and is set to a playful text, one that undoubtedly has double meanings. In addition, the structure of the music has identical and near-identical repeated sections, syncopations, and a brief section of triple meter. The reference to "None" is to the ninth hour of the daily offices of the Roman Catholic Church.

All day long you tell me, sing, sing, but don't you see that I'm out of breath? Why so much singing? I wish you would tell me, play, play, not the bells at None, but on your cembalo. Oh, if I survive the scra-scra-scratching, let me hold you in my clutches.

28. JACOB HANDL—*PATER NOSTER*

Handl's setting of the Lord's Prayer is one of the most celebrated motets of the composer and of the late Renaissance era. It is in the polychoral dialogue style, with numerous exchanges between the upper and lower voices (note especially measures 27–36 and 65–69), and is basically homophonic in texture; examples of imitative polyphony are brief and only pervasive among all the voice parts at the Amen text. Moreover, the text setting is almost entirely syllabic, with careful attention to natural speech declamation and with tonal cadences at the ends of important phrases. The text is from Matthew 6:9–13.

Our father, who is in heaven, your name is sanctified; let your kingdom come, and be done of your will, on earth as it is in heaven. Give us our daily bread today, and forgive us our debts just as we forgive our debtors; and lead us not into temptation, but deliver us from the evil one. Amen.

29. HANS LEO HASSLER—*DIXIT MARIA*

Although Hassler was born and worked in Germany and although he composed notable motets and lieder to German texts, he is best known for his Latin motets. *Dixit Maria* is in the point-of-imitation style, with brief sections of homophony—this mixture of imitative polyphony and homophony being popular throughout Europe during the middle and late years of the Renaissance era. The initial point of imitation occupies the first half of the motet, while the following and final point, which begins with a short homophonic passage and is repeated, occupies the motet's second half. The structure of the motet is therefore ABB. The text is from Luke 1: 38.

Mary said to the angel: Behold the handmaid of the Lord; be it done to me according to your word.

30. MICHAEL PRAETORIUS—*ES IST EIN ROS ENTSPRUNGEN*

The tune that Praetorius set was familiar to both Roman Catholics and German Protestants at the end of the Renaissance era: it appeared with twenty-three verses in the *Alte Catholische geistliche Kirchengeseng* (Old Catholic Hymnal) of 1599 and the *Speirschen Gesenbuch* (Speyer Hymnal) of 1600. Praetorius made his setting approximately a decade later and included it in the sixth volume of his *Musae Sioniae* published in 1609. The form of the setting is chorale-like, with a homophonic texture, an AAB strophic structure, and a prominent melody in the top voice part. Two verses are included in the edition published here, with a third verse printed below.

1. *A rose has sprung forth from a tender root, as the old ones [prophets] sang to us, from Jesse came the lineage; and it has brought a little flower, in the middle of cold winter, right at half night.*
2. *The little rose, the one that I mean, about which Isaiah spoke, has been brought to us alone by Mary, the pure maiden; from God's eternal counsel, she has borne a child and has remained a pure virgin.*
3. *The little flower so small, it smells to us so sweet; with his bright light he dispels the darkness. True human and true God, help us from all suffering, deliver us from sin and death.*

31. MELCHIOR FRANCK—*MEINE SCHWESTER, LIEBE BRAUT*

Published in *Geistliche Gesäng und Melodeyen* in 1608, Franck's motet is in a style typical during the latter years of the Renaissance era in Germany: the texture is basically homophonic, text phrases are presented with little repetition and in rhythmic patterns that emulate natural speech declamation, and key words are set to melodic and rhythmic shapes that pictorialize their meanings—for example, the rising and falling pattern to the word "Quellen" (fountain), the command-like setting of "Steh auf, Nordwind" (Awake, North Wind), and the melismatic treatment of "wehe" (blow). The text is from the Song of Solomon 4:12–16.

My sister, dear bride, you are a sequestered garden, a sealed fountain, an enclosed spring. Your plants are as a pleasure garden of pomegranates with precious fruits, henna with spikenard, spikenard with saffron, calamus and cinnamon, with all kinds of trees of frankincense, myrrh and aloes, with all the finest spices, like a garden spring, like a spring of living water that flows from Lebanon. Awake North Wind, and come South Wind, and blow through my garden, that its spices may flow out.

32. THOMAS TALLIS—*IF YE LOVE ME*

If ye love me is an example of the early anthems composed for the Anglican Church in England: the anthems are short in duration, the scoring is economical (generally for only four voice parts), the textures alternate between homophony and simple imitative polyphony, and the text settings are syllabic. In addition, there are often sectional repeats (resulting in an ABB form in the case of *If ye love me*). The edition here is scored in its original version for men's voices (male alto, tenors, and bass). The text is from John 14:15–17.

33. WILLIAM BYRD—*AVE VERUM CORPUS*

Byrd's Latin motet, certainly the most famous of his sacred works, was published in 1605 in a collection of pieces entitled *Gradualia ac cantiones sacrae*. These pieces, as well as those in a companion publication of 1607 entitled *Gradualia seu cantionum sacrarum, liber secundus*, were designed to be sung in private Catholic services on the major feast days of the liturgical year. The basic homophonic texture of *Ave verum corpus*, as well as its formal structure of AAB, reflect Byrd's writing for limited and amateur musical resources. The text is a sequence hymn for the Feast of Corpus Christi.

Hail, true body, born of the Virgin Mary, who truly suffered, sacrificed on the cross for mankind; whose side was pierced, blood flowing like water; be for us a cupbearer when in death we are judged. Oh sweetness, oh holiness, oh Jesus son of Mary, have mercy on me. Amen.

34. THOMAS MORLEY—*MY BONNY LASS SHE SMILETH*

One of Morley's best-known compositions in one of his favorite genres, *My bonny lass she smileth* was published in *The First Book of Balletts to Five Voices* (1595). This collection is a close copy of Giovanni Giacomo Gastoldi's *Balletti* of 1591, not only with an identical number and layout of pieces, but also with identical formal structures of the pieces (AABB with "fa la la" refrains) and with virtual translations of eight of Gastoldi's poems, including *My bonny lass she smileth* (which was *Questa dolce sirena*), *Sing we and chant it* (from *A lieta vita*), and *Shoot, false love, I care not* (from *Viver lieto voglio*).

35. JOHN DOWLAND—*NOW, OH NOW, I NEEDS MUST PART*

Dowland's more than eighty lute songs were published in three books. The first book, which contains *Now, oh now, I needs must part* (subtitled "The Frog Galliard"), was published in 1597 and was so popular it went through four reprintings in the following decade. The full title of the book—*The First Booke of Songs or Ayres of fowre partes wth Tableture for the Lute: So made that all the partes together, or either of them severally may be sung to the Lute, Orpherian or Viol de gambo*—provides an indication of the varying performance practices of the songs, which were generally performed either by a solo voice singing the top part with accompaniment of a lute or lute-like instrument such as the orpharion, or by four voices singing all the parts, with or without accompaniment of lute and/or a bass instrument. All the songs are strophic and contain from two to six verses.

36. THOMAS TOMKINS—*O PRAY FOR THE PEACE OF JERUSALEM*

This is an example of the early English anthem as it emulated the point-of-imitation Latin motet: each phrase of text is treated imitatively throughout all the voice parts. The anthem is generally shorter, however, with fewer lines of text, and the harmonic language is more tonal. A number of the anthems are also scored to take advantage of the divided choral forces typical in Anglican churches; the right side of the ensemble is called *decani* (indicating the side of the church where the dean sits) and the left side is called *cantoris* (the cantor's side). In *O pray for the peace of Jerusalem*, the top two voice parts are for *decani* and *cantoris* treble voices and are of equal range; the anthem has no alto part.

37. JOHN WILBYE—*FLORA GAVE ME FAIREST FLOWERS*

Generally acknowledged to be Wilbye's most popular composition, *Flora gave me fairest-flowers* is illustrative of the English canzonet at the end of the sixteenth century. With a lighthearted text and a basically homophonic texture, the canzonet was in contrast to the madrigal, which was most often set to a more serious text with longer point-of-imitation phrases. Wilbye's canzonet also illustrates the harmonically tonal characteristic of canzonets.

38. Thomas Weelkes—*When David heard that Absalom was slain*

Generally acknowledged as one of the most artistically superior compositions of the English Renaissance, *When David heard that Absalom was slain* is difficult to identify in terms of genre classification. With its long points of imitation, it is not typical of the anthems in England during the late Renaissance. On the other hand, it is not a typical madrigal since it wasn't published as such and since it has a sacred text (from 2 Samuel 18:33). Given its madrigalistic characteristics, however, especially its text painting of "he went up" and the two simultaneous cross relations that characterize the climax of the phrase "would God I had died for thee," it is probably best described as a spiritual madrigal. In terms of scoring, it should be noted that the two soprano and two alto parts are equal in range and that each part crosses over the other frequently.

39. Orlando Gibbons—*Almighty and everlasting God*

This is an example of a "full anthem" (scored entirely for choral forces), which is in contrast to the "verse anthem" (scored for a combination of choral and solo forces). It is also an example of small-scale anthems that emulated the Palestrinian motet style fashionable in Italy during the latter part of the Renaissance era: phrases are of balanced length and are treated imitatively in each voice part. *Almighty and everlasting God* is structured of four relatively equal phrases (each treated as a point of imitation) and a short closing coda.

40. Claudio Monteverdi—*Confitebor secondo*

This is one of numerous psalm settings composed by Monteverdi and contained in a publication entitled *Selva morale e spirituale*, published in 1640. Most of the settings, as here, are scored for voices, two violins, and basso continuo. The reference to "secondo" in the title distinguishes this setting from another one set to the same text (Psalm 111). The music is characterized by the repetition of short ostinato-like musical phrases and by concertato dialogue between the voices and violins.

I acknowledge you Lord with my whole heart, in the council of the just and in the congregation. Great are the Lord's works, chosen by his desires. I acknowledge the magnificence of his deeds and his justice endures forever and ever. He has made memorials of his miracles, a merciful and compassionate Lord. He feeds those who fear him, he will remember forever his covenant. The power of his works will be announced to his people, so that he may give them the inheritance of the nations. The works of his hands are truth and justice, all his commandments are true, confirmed forever and ever, made in truth and fairness. The Lord has saved his people, he has given his pledge forever, holy and awesome is his name. The fear of the Lord is the beginning of wisdom, all who practice it understand well, his praise endures forever. Glory to the father and son and holy spirit, as it was in the beginning, is now and always, forever and ever. Amen.

41. Claudio Monteverdi—*Sfogava con le stelle*

This madrigal comes from the fourth of eight books of madrigals composed by Monteverdi. Published in 1603, at the very beginning of the Baroque era, book 4 is transitional in nature and contains examples of Renaissance polyphony as well as numerous examples of highly expressive and speech-like settings of text. In *Sfogava con le stelle*, for example, there are seven passages of music and text that have no rhythmic notation, but instead are free—to be sung as in natural speech or as in recitative, which was a hallmark of the new Baroque operatic style.

Together with the stars, a man sick with love under a night sky poured out his sorrow, and said, gazing upon them: Oh lovely images of the idol whom I adore. Just as you show me, while thus you shine, her rare beauty, so show to her my own feelings of passion. Make her, with your golden likenesses, merciful, yes, as you make me a lover.

42. Giacomo Carissimi—*Jonas* (Peccavimus Domine)

Jonas is one of approximately eleven oratorios composed by Carissimi. Most of them, establishing the model of the oratorio during all later historical eras, are settings in Latin of stories that depict events in the life of Old Testament characters. Carissimi's *Jonas*, for instance, tells the story of Jonah, who is caught in a violent storm at sea, thrown overboard, swallowed and regurgitated by a whale, and sent to redeem the people of Nineveh. The chorus printed here closes the oratorio and represents the response of the Ninevites. The music of the oratorio is typical of that composed at the beginning of the Baroque era: scoring is for voices and basso continuo, and most of the text is related through recitative and descriptive choruses.

We have sinned, Lord, and have not walked in your ways; but turn around, Lord, and let us turn back; illuminate your face and we will be saved.

43. ALESSANDRO SCARLATTI—*MESSA DI S CECILIA* (SANCTUS)

Alessandro Scarlatti, father of the keyboard composer Domenico, is known mostly for his oratorios (he composed thirty-eight of them). However, he also wrote ten masses and more than one hundred motets. His early masses are in the Renaissance *prima prattica* style, called by Scarlatti "alla Palestrina." The later masses, including *Messa di S Cecilia*, are in the Baroque *seconda prattica* style, scored for soloists, chorus, strings, and basso continuo, and characterized by figural patterns for both the chorus and instruments. In addition, as seen in the Sanctus, the voices alternate between passages of homophony and melismatic duets.

Holy, holy, holy, Lord God of hosts. Heaven and earth are full of your glory. Hosanna in the highest. Blessed is he who comes in the name of the Lord. Hosanna in the highest.

44. ANTONIO LOTTI—*CRUCIFIXUS*

Lotti composed three settings of the Crucifixus text from the Roman Catholic Mass Ordinary. The setting here, his most famous, was originally the second section of his *Credo* in F Major. In this larger setting, the *Crucifixus* is scored for voices and instruments *colla parte*. The music is in the form of a Renaissance motet, with each phrase of text treated imitatively throughout all the voice parts. However, the harmonic texture is Baroque in nature and characterized by Lotti's penchant for melodic suspensions.

He was crucified also for us under Pontius Pilate, suffered, and was buried.

45. ANTONIO VIVALDI—*GLORIA* RV589 (ET IN TERRA PAX)

Included in the several mass movements composed by Vivaldi are two settings of the Gloria text. The first, with the catalog number RV589, is the most popular, while the second (RV588), which is almost identical to the first, is nowadays hardly known. In both works "Et in terra pax" is the second of twelve movements. Its instrumental texture is characterized by imitative passages over repeated-note bass parts, while its vocal texture is basically one long point of imitation, replete with rising chromatic patterns and melodic suspensions that were favored during the Baroque era.

And on earth peace to men of goodwill.

46. MARC-ANTOINE CHARPENTIER—*IN NATIVITATEM DOMINI CANTICUM*, H314

Of Charpentier's twenty-two oratorios, seven are set to texts about the Christmas story, and of these, H314 (printed here) and H416 have identical titles. In addition, the title of H414 is almost identical (*In nativitatem Domini nostri Jesus Christi canticum*). All the French Christmas oratorios are referred to as pastorales, mostly because they contain texts that focus on the announcement of Christ's birth to the shepherds. In addition, pastorales do not relate typical Old Testament stories, and the text is not set to a preponderance of recitatives. In Charpentier's H314, for instance, the text is delivered by alternating sections of choruses and short ariosos sung by a solo bass.

Whom did you see, shepherds, tell us, proclaim to us, who has appeared on earth? We saw the newborn from the virgin, the son who is given to us, and choirs of angels praising him. The Lord has made known his salvation, and has revealed his justice in all the earth. Sing praises to the Lord on the cithara and with the voice of a psalm, on the metal trumpet and horn. The rivers will clap their hands and the mountains rejoice at his sight, for he has come to save the earth.

47. Michel-Richard de Lalande—*Super flumina Babylonis* (Hymnum cantate nobis)

Lalande was famous for his grand motets, which were popular at the court of Louis XIV and were performed frequently by concert societies throughout France. All of the works in the genre were large-scale, divided into numerous movements, and scored for soloists, chorus, and instruments. Lalande's *Super flumina Babylonis*, composed in 1687, is divided into twelve movements—seven for soloists (including several duets and trios) and five for chorus alone or for chorus and soloists. "Hymnum cantate nobis," for bass solo and chorus, is the fourth movement.

We sing hymns from the songs of Zion.

48. Heinrich Schütz—*Musicalische Exequien* (Herr, wenn ich nur dich habe)

This motet is the second movement of *Musicalische Exequien* (Musical Obsequies or Funeral Rites), which Schütz composed in 1636 for the funeral of his patron, Prince von Reuss. All the movements are in the Baroque concerted style (Schütz even called the movements "concerted works"). Movement 1 is in the form of a German missa, with alternating sections of music for various solo combinations and chorus. Movement 2 is in the Venetian polychoral style that Schütz favored throughout his life; the two choruses are in dialogue with each other throughout the composition, exchanging and alternating long phrases and short motifs, all set in rhythmic patterns that mirror natural spoken declamation. The third movement is also polychoral, but here the two choruses have different texts—the first "Herr, nun lässest du deinen Diener" (Lord, now let your servant depart in peace) and the second "Selig sind die Toten" (Blessed are the dead). The text for movement 2 is from Psalm 73:25–26.

Lord, if I have but you, I ask not for heaven or for earth. When my body and my heart fail, then are you, God, forever my heart's strength and my portion.

49. SAMUEL SCHEIDT—*ANGELUS AD PASTORES AIT,* SSWV13

Although the majority of Scheidt's compositions are German motets (he composed almost 150 of them), he is most known today for his Latin motets (of which he composed twenty-eight). These are mainly in a *prima prattica* Renaissance style, with fragments of text treated imitatively. However, as seen in *Angelus ad pastores ait,* Scheidt composed in a Venetian polychoral style as well. Here, Renaissance dialogue textures alternate with Baroque-style figural exchanges for the two soprano parts and for the sopranos and altos in duet. The texture is also varied to include meter changes and a section of homophony.

The angel said to the shepherds: I announce to you great joy, because born to you today is the savior of the world. Alleluia.

50. DIETRICH BUXTEHUDE—*DAS NEUGEBOR'NE KINDELEIN,* BUXWV13

Buxtehude is known for establishing the cantata as a sacred choral genre when previously it had been a setting of secular texts scored for soloists. Most of his more than one hundred cantatas are scored for three or four voice parts, strings, and basso continuo, and in addition, most are divided into sections that are delineated by tempo changes. In *Das neugebor'ne Kindelein,* the strings appear alone at the beginning of the cantata as an introduction and as interludes between sentences of text. Also, the chorus and strings often participate in a dialogue of motivic material, and tempo changes underscore the expressive content of the text.

The newborn child, the dearly loved little Jesus, brings again a new year to the chosen Christian flock. At this the little angels rejoice, who gladly are around with us, and sing in the air so free, that God is reconciled with us. Since God is reconciled and our friend, what can the evil foe do to us? Despite the devil, world, and hell's gate, the little Jesus is our refuge. He brings the true year of jubilation, so why do we always mourn? Take heart, it is now time for singing: the little Jesus averts all suffering.

51. JOHANN LUDWIG BACH—*DAS IST MEINE FREUDE*

This motet, composed by Johann Sebastian Bach's third cousin, is typical of the genre during the Baroque era in Germany: the scoring is for double chorus; the texture is polychoral, with exchanges of motivic material between the two choruses; the melodies contain passages of melismas used as word painting; and meter and tempo are varied to delineate changes in text expression. *Das ist meine Freude*, one of the most popular German motets of the Baroque, is notable for its repetition of the text's first word, by short motivic passages in dialogue between the two choruses, and by melismas that are set to the word "Freude" (joy). The text is from Psalm 73:28.

This is my joy, that I stay close to God and place my confidence in the Lord.

52. GEORG PHILIPP TELEMANN—*UNS IST EIN KIND GEBOREN*, TWV1:1451 (MOVEMENT 1)

Telemann's more than one thousand sacred cantatas range from small-scale pieces for solo voices and a few instruments to multimovement works scored for soloists, chorus, and large instrumental ensembles. *Uns ist ein Kind geboren* is one of the large-scale works. Its eight movements include three arias, one duet, one recitative, two choruses, and one chorale. Instrumental scoring is for trumpets, timpani, oboes, strings, and basso continuo. The choruses, as represented by movement 1 here, are expository in nature and are unified in both choral and instrumental textures by motivic material that generally contains expressive melismatic passages.

For us a child is born, a son is given to us.

53. JOHANN SEBASTIAN BACH—*B MINOR MASS* (ET INCARNATUS EST, CRUCIFIXUS, AND ET RESURREXIT)

The three movements printed here are from the Symbolum Nicenum (Credo) of the *B Minor Mass* and illustrate Bach's masterful treatment of the two main compositional styles employed in this monumental work. The "Et incarnatus est" and "Crucifixus" are in a neo-Renaissance *prima prattica* style, with minimal scoring for instruments and with the main phrases of text treated in a point-of-imitation fashion. The "Et resurrexit" is in the Baroque *concertato* style, with significant scoring for instruments and with alternation of extended choral and orchestral passages. In addition, the "Et resurrexit" features long melismas, a solo passage for bass and instruments, and dense textures. The tempos of all three movements are dictated by the meter signatures and the expressive nature of the texts. Of significance, the 3/2 meter during Bach's time indicated a very slow tempo, while 3/4 indicated a medium tempo, and 3/8 indicated a fast tempo.

And was made flesh by the holy spirit of the Virgin Mary, and was made man. He was crucified also for us under Pontius Pilate, suffered, and was buried. And he rose on the third day according to scriptures; and he ascended to heaven, sits at the right hand of God the father, and he will come again with glory to judge the living and dead, whose kingdom will have no end.

54. JOHANN SEBASTIAN BACH—*PASSIO SECUNDUM JOHANNEN* (RUHT WOHL AND ACH HERR, LASS DEIN LIEB ENGELEIN)

The two movements printed here are at the end of Bach's *St. John Passion*. "Ruht wohl" fulfills the role of the traditional *Schlusschor*—a chorus that closes many German passion oratorios and that, with a nonbiblical poetic text, comments on the significance of the passion story. The form of the movement is ABA: the initial A begins and ends with identical statements of orchestral material; the beginning and end of the B section are almost identical; the middle of the B section is built on material from A; and the final A is a da capo of the first A. The movement is, therefore, in a mirror arrangement—a common form for Bach. "Ach Herr, lass dein lieb Engelein" is a Lutheran chorale and also fulfills a concluding role in that chorales were often used to close the first half of German oratorios and in that they generally commented on the passion story in a way that made it relevant to contemporary people. The form of the chorale is in a traditional AAB arrangement: the A portion is the *Stollen* and the B portion the *Abgesang*. Bach's *St. John Passion* is unique in ending with both a *Schlusschor* and a chorale.

Rest well, you sacred limbs, I will no longer weep for you, rest well and bring me also to rest. The grave, that is allotted to you and that contains no further suffering, opens heaven for me and shuts off hell.

Oh Lord, let your dear angels at my final hour carry my soul to Abraham's bosom, while my body in its narrow chamber gently without pain or torment rests until the last day. Wake me then from death, so that my eyes see you in all joy, oh God's son, my savior and throne of mercy. Lord Jesus Christ, hear me, I will praise you eternally.

55. JOHN BLOW—*SALVATOR MUNDI*

Although Blow composed more than one hundred anthems and ten Anglican services, he is best-known today for one of his two Latin motets—*Salvator mundi*. Typical of the genre during the early Baroque, it is in a Renaissance *prima prattica* style, with imitative phrases pervading the vocal texture. However, Blow also incorporates a number of Baroque traits, including an independent basso continuo line, short motivic imitative phrases, and repetition of notes (seen in the first phrase). The text is from an antiphon for Holy Unction in the *Book of Common Prayer*.

Savior of the world, save us, who by the cross and blood redeemed us, help us, we pray to you, our God.

56. HENRY PURCELL—*REMEMBER NOT, LORD, OUR OFFENCES*

This anthem, undoubtedly Purcell's most famous, is representative of the full anthem during the early years of the Baroque era in England. The texture consists of alternating sections of homophony and simple polyphony, the harmonic language is diatonic, the length of the anthem is short, and the scoring is for a cappella chorus, although use of organ *colla parte* was common at the time. The two soprano parts occupy the same range and are an indication of the typical arrangement of choral forces in Anglican churches: divided and facing each other, one half of the ensemble is referred to as *cantoris* (the cantor's side of the church), while the other half of the ensemble is called the *decani* (the dean's side of the church). The text is from the Litany in the *Book of Common Prayer*.

57. GEORGE FRIDERIC HANDEL—*SAUL* (HOW EXCELLENT THY NAME, O LORD)

Saul, composed during the late summer of 1738 and premiered in January of 1739, is considered to be Handel's first great oratorio. It was immensely popular during its day and was the most frequently performed of Handel's oratorios during the nineteenth century. (*Messiah*, composed three years after *Saul*, was more popular during the twentieth century.) The libretto of *Saul*, written by Charles Jennens, who was also the librettist for *Messiah* and two other Handel oratorios, relates the biblical story of Saul from 1 Samuel. The chorus "How excellent thy name, O Lord" occurs twice in the oratorio—at the beginning and end of Scene 1 (the music printed here is the second of the occurrences). The entire scene, indicated in the libretto as sung by a "Chorus of Israelites," is subtitled "An Epinicion or Song of Triumph for the victory over Goliath and the Philistines." The music is typical of Handel's writing in other celebratory choruses: the scoring includes trumpets and timpani, the texture alternates between homophonic and imitative sections, and there are melismatic passages for both chorus and orchestra.

58. MAURICE GREENE—*LORD, LET ME KNOW MINE END*

This is an example of a late-Baroque English verse anthem, categorized as such because of the scoring for an independent accompaniment and for both choral and solo voices. The basso continuo line would most likely have been realized on the organ, and the treble parts at the center of the anthem would have been sung by soloists—one each from the *cantoris* and *decani* sides of the choir. The texture of the music is in a Renaissance *prima prattica* style, characterized by continuous points of imitation that alternate with brief passages of homophony, but with the Baroque predilection for syllabic text setting and short phrases. The text is from Psalm 39:4–7 and is intended for use at funerals.

59. Juan Gutiérrez de Padilla—*Versa est in luctum*

This is an example of the Latin motet as it existed in the New World (Mexico and South America) during the Baroque era. The textures are in a Renaissance *prima prattica* style, with alternating imitative and homophonic phrases, and in addition there is no scoring for basso continuo or other instruments. Other Renaissance traits include manipulation of melodic material, such as can be seen with the inversion of intervals in the first soprano and altos lines at the beginning of *Versa est in luctum*. This melodic treatment is also an example of Padilla's expressive word painting (the harp being turned to mourning). The text is from Job 30:31.

My harp is turned to mourning, and my music into the voice of weeping. Spare me, Lord, for my days are nothing.

60. Ignacio Jerusalem—*Responsorio sequndo de SS José*

Jerusalem, also known by Jerusalem Stella, composed eleven sets of responsories for the Mexico City Cathedral, where he was *maestro de capilla* from 1750 until his death in 1769. The scoring for most of these works is for soloists, chorus, and large instrumental ensemble, and the style, as seen in this "Second Responsory for St. Joseph," is mainly *galant*, with textures that are predominately homophonic and chordal, and rhythms and harmonies that are direct and uncomplicated. The text is from Genesis 41:55–56.

When famine was in the land of Egypt, the people cried to the pharaoh for bread and he responded: Go to Joseph, and do what he tells you. When the famine had spread over the entire land, Joseph opened the storehouses and sold grain to the Egyptians.

61. Joseph Haydn—*The Creation* (Achieved is the glorious work)

The Creation, Haydn's second oratorio, was composed between 1796 and 1798 and premiered in April of 1798. Its success was immediate, and it has become one of the most popular and frequently performed choral/orchestral works in the history of music. Haydn modeled the structural organization and details of his work on Handel oratorios, which he first heard at Handel commemoration concerts in London in 1791. For instance, Haydn's oratorio is divided into three large parts, there are frequent instances of highly descriptive word painting, numerous choruses are significant in the development of the story, and the choruses emulate Handelian textures and structures. In addition, the libretto, based on Milton's *Paradise Lost*, presumably was originally written for Handel. Haydn had it translated into German and upon finishing the oratorio (called *Die Schöpfung*) had the text immediately retranslated back to English. When the score was first published in 1800, it contained both German and English texts. "Achieved is the glorious work," which is often extracted and performed separately, ends the second part of the oratorio—the completion of the sixth day of creation.

62. MICHAEL HAYDN—*SALVE REGINA*, MH634

More prolific than his older brother Joseph, Michael's compositional output includes approximately thirty-five masses, six oratorios, and over four hundred motets. The motets are divided into two stylistic groups—old and new. The motets in the older style emulate the a cappella imitative *prima prattica* textures of the Renaissance, while the motets in the newer style, as represented by *Salve regina* printed here, have choral textures that are basically homophonic, with more elaborate compositional material scored for instruments—generally horns, strings, and basso continuo. The text is the same as that of #1.

63. WOLFGANG AMADEUS MOZART—*REQUIEM* (LACRIMOSA)

Mozart's *Requiem* is one of the most enigmatic compositions in the history of Western music, well-known because of its popularity and frequency of performance, but little-known for circumstances related to its authorship. Especially perplexing is the uncertainty regarding the portions of the work actually composed by Mozart and the identity of the composer of the remaining portions. It is generally assumed that Mozart wrote and partially scored the music of the work's first three movements, up to and including the first eight measures of the "Lacrimosa," which is the sixth and final portion of movement 3—the sequence called the Dies irae. The music of the "Lacrimosa," which is perhaps the most recognizable section of the *Requiem*, is characterized by a pervasive undulating violin melody that serves as an obbligato to the basically homophonic choral texture and also as an expressive manifestation of the text.

How tearful that day on which the guilty man will rise from embers to be judged. Spare him then, God. Merciful Lord Jesus, grant them rest.

64. FRANZ SCHUBERT—*DIE NACHT*

Most of Schubert's more than seventy part songs were composed for male voices—ensembles of men organized into singing societies that were popular throughout Austria during the early years of the nineteenth century. The texture of the repertoire composed for these ensembles is generally homophonic, and, as seen in *Die Nacht*, the form is basically strophic.

How beautiful you are, friendly stillness, heavenly peace. See how the clear stars move in the heaven's meadows, and look down on us, silently from the blue distance. Silently approaches the mildness of spring to the soft lap of earth, adorning the silvery spring with moss and the plains with flowers.

65. LUIGI CHERUBINI—*REQUIEM* IN C MINOR (GRADUALE)

Of Cherubini's twelve surviving masses, two are Requiems—one in C Minor, composed in 1816 to commemorate the anniversary of the execution of Louis XVI, and one in D Minor, composed in 1836 for intended use at Cherubini's own funeral. The first of the Requiem settings, the more expansive, is scored for mixed chorus and orchestra consisting of oboes, clarinets, bassoons, horns, trumpets, trombones, timpani, tam-tam, and strings. The Graduale from this Requiem, which is the second of the work's seven movements, is scored for chorus and only violas, cellos, and basses. The texture of the choral writing is an imitative duet for the major part of the movement, the sopranos and tenors in dialogue with the altos and basses.

Rest eternal grant them, Lord, and let perpetual light shine on them. The just man will be remembered forever, he will not fear hearing evil.

66. GIOACHINO ROSSINI—*STABAT MATER* (INTRODUZIONE)

Rossini's compositional output consists mostly of operas, all of which were composed during the first half of his life (he had composed forty operas by the time he was thirty-seven). He wrote mostly small-scale vocal and instrumental works during the remaining years of his life, with the exception of two large-scale choral works—the *Stabat mater* between 1832 and 1842 and the *Petite messe solennelle* in 1864 (revised in 1867). The *Stabat mater* is a cantata-like work in ten movements, all of which involve soloists except for movements 5 and 10. The first movement, printed here, is for solo quartet and chorus, with a brief section for solo tenor in the middle portion of the movement. The instrumental scoring represents what would become the standard in full orchestras—flutes, oboes, clarinets, bassoons, horns, trumpets, trombones, timpani, and strings.

The sorrowful mother stood weeping beside the cross where her son was hanging.

67. WILLIAM BILLINGS—*CHESTER*

Billings composed more than two hundred hymns, most of which were given place-names (e.g., Nantucket, Hampshire, Cambridge, and Chester) that had no particular relevance to the hymn texts, although the texts, as seen below, occasionally make reference to events and people in

New England. The melody of the hymns was placed in the tenor voice part, with performance of the soprano and tenor parts sung by both males and females. The texture of the music is homophonic and the form strophic. The first and final verses are printed with the music, while all five verses, presumably written by Billings himself, are printed here.

1. *Let tyrants shake their iron rod, and slav'ry clank her galling chains, we fear them not, we trust in God, New England's God forever reigns.*
2. *Howe and Burgoyne and Clinton too, with Prescott and Cornwallis join'd, together plot our over-throw, in one infernal league combin'd.*
3. *When God inspir'd us for the fight, their ranks were broke, their lines were forc'd, their ships were shatter'd in our sight, or swiftly driven from our coast.*
4. *The foe comes on with haughty stride, our troops advance with martial noise, their vet'rans flee before our youth, and gen'rals yield to beardless boys.*
5. *What grateful off'ring shall we bring? What shall we render to the Lord? Loud Halleluiahs let us sing, and praise his name on ev'ry chord.*

68. HECTOR BERLIOZ—*LA DAMNATION DE FAUST* (APOTHÉOSE DE MARGUERITE)

The secular choral/orchestral works of Berlioz are difficult to categorize, in large part because they do not conform to well-established genres and because Berlioz described them in new, unique ways. *La damnation de Faust*, for example, was labeled a "légende dramatique" (dramatic legend). The work has all the characteristics of an oratorio, however (a narrative story of an historic figure related through recitatives, solo passages, and choruses), and is usually referred to as such. The Apothéose de Marguerite is the final scene of the work, which represents the forgiveness of Marguerite and depicts her ascent into heaven. The scoring is indicative of the creative and extravagant nature of Berlioz, who calls for eight to ten harps that play from two parts and a children's chorus ad libitum that sings from the soprano solo part.

Rise up to heaven, naive soul, that love led astray. Return to your original beauty that an error altered. Come, the heavenly virgins, your sisters, the seraphim, will dry the tears that earthly sorrows still exact. Hope on and smile on your blessings. Come, Marguerite.

69. CAMILLE SAINT-SAËNS—*CALME DE NUITS*

While Saint-Saëns is known mainly for his instrumental compositions and the opera *Samson et Dalila*, he composed a number of choral works, including forty secular cantatas and part songs for the many choral societies that were popular in France during his lifetime. Many of the part songs were scored for men's voices, and their considerable vocal challenges testify to the high level of amateur singing in France. *Calme de nuits*, published with *Les fleurs et les arbres* as op. 68, is scored for mixed voices a cappella and represents Saint-Saëns's simple though highly effective style. The texture is predominately homophonic, and the harmonic language is simple and direct.

The calm of night, the freshness of evening, the vast shimmering of the spheres, the great silence of black caverns, you enchant every thoughtful soul. The bright sun, merriment, and noise, you bring fleeting joy; only the poet is haunted by his love of quiet things.

70. GABRIEL FAURÉ—*REQUIEM* (AGNUS DEI)

During the six-year compositional history of the *Requiem*, Fauré made a number of changes in both content and orchestration. The mass began and was performed as a five-movement work (Introit and Kyrie, Sanctus, Pie Jesu, Agnus Dei and Communion, and In paradisum) scored for solo soprano, mixed chorus, and a small number of instruments. The final and published version included two more movements (the Offertory and Libera me) and scoring for full orchestra. This orchestration was most likely not done by Fauré, however, who preferred the more intimate, chamber-like setting. The Agnus Dei, which became the fourth movement of the *Requiem*, has an ABACDA structure: the first and second A sections feature the choral tenors alone; the B and C sections are for chorus, with the B section in the tonic key of F Major and the C section in A-flat Major; the D section has music and text from the beginning of movement one; and the final A section recapitulates the movement's opening orchestral material.

Lamb of God, who takes away the sins of the world, grant them rest forever. May eternal light shine on them, Lord, with your saints forever, for you are merciful. Grant eternal rest to them, Lord, and let perpetual light shine on them.

71. GIUSEPPE VERDI—*MESSA DA REQUIEM* (SANCTUS)

Verdi began thinking about composing a Requiem in 1868, four days after the death of Gioachino Rossini. This Requiem was to be a composite work by thirteen Italian composers, Verdi writing the last movement (Libera me). Troubles plagued the process, and the work was not performed as planned. But after the death of Italy's beloved poet Alessandro Manzoni in 1873, Verdi decided to compose his own complete Requiem, which he did and which was performed a year later on the first anniversary of the poet's death. This work, while notable for its operatic writing and many expressive and dramatic passages, is also remarkable for its many balanced structural elements. The entire work, for example, centers around the Sanctus, which is the only movement not scored for soloists and which is structured as a double fugue framed by a short introduction and a closing. The text is the same as that of #43.

72. Ludwig van Beethoven—*Missa* in C Major, op. 86 (Kyrie)

The *Missa* in C Major is the result of a commission Beethoven received from Prince Nikolaus Esterházy in 1807 to compose a mass in celebration of the name day of the prince's wife. This commission followed and was to be in the tradition of the six masses Joseph Haydn had composed for the princess between 1796 and 1802. Beethoven's mass is similar to Haydn's masses in structure and design: the vocal scoring is for standard SATB chorus and SATB soloists generally scored in a quartet texture; the orchestral scoring is the same as in Haydn's final mass; the movements of both masses are structured similarly, with the Gloria and Credo divided into three parts; and the two masses are approximately the same length. However, as noted by the wide range of expressive markings, Beethoven's mass is more dramatic. The Kyrie, for example, has ten Italian words at the beginning of the movement that attempt to create a specific expressive quality: "Andante con moto assai vivace quasi allegretto ma non troppo" (A walking tempo with motion and very vivacious as an allegretto but not too much). The music of this Kyrie also returns at the end of the mass. The text is the same as that of #3.

73. Felix Mendelssohn—*Elias* (Siehe, der Hüter Israels) / *Elijah* (He, watching over Israel)

Mendelssohn was a highly respected and active conductor during his lifetime, leading numerous performances of oratorios, including Handel's *Messiah* and *Judas Maccabaeus*, J. S. Bach's *St. Matthew Passion*, and Joseph Haydn's *The Creation*. These oratorios were the models for Mendelssohn's two oratorios—*Paulus*, composed from 1834 to 1836, and *Elijah*, composed in 1846. Both works are an amalgamation of elements from traditional English oratorios (with recitatives, arias, and choruses) and from German Lutheran Passions (with chorales). *Elijah* was a commission from the Birmingham Festival, and although Mendelssohn originally set the text in German, he supervised its translation into English, which was the language of the premiere performance and all subsequent performances he conducted. "He, watching over Israel" (Siehe, der Hüter Israels) is in part 2 of the oratorio, at the place in the story when Elijah is asleep in the wilderness and angels sing over him. The structure of the movement is Handelian: a melody is stated and developed, another melody follows and is treated similarly, then both melodies are combined and developed.

74. Robert Schumann—*Minnespiel*, op. 101 (So wahr die Sonne scheinet)

Schumann composed several cycles of vocal chamber music similar in design to the *Liebeslieder Walzer*, op. 52, and *Neue Liebeslieder Walzer*, op. 65, by Johannes Brahms; all the cycles consist of solo songs, duets, and vocal quartets accompanied by piano. Schumann's three cycles, *Spanisches Liederspiel, Spanische Liebeslieder,* and *Minnespiel,* were composed in 1849, the year after he founded the Dresden Verein für Chorgesang. *Minnespiel* contains eight pieces (three solos, three duets, and two quartets), with "Schön ist das Fest des Lenzes" (Beautiful is the festival of spring) serving as the fifth piece and "So wahr die Sonne scheinet" ending the cycle. The several solo lines in this latter piece indicate and highlight the vocal chamber nature of the entire cycle.

As truly as the sun shines, as truly as the flames spark, as truly as the clouds weep, as truly as spring blooms, as truly as I felt as I held you in my embrace, you love me, as I love you, I love you, as you love me. The sun may stop shining, the clouds may no longer weep, the flames may die down, spring may no longer blossom, but we will embrace each other and feel this way forever; you love me, as I love you, I love you, as you love me.

75. FRANZ LISZT—*AVE VERUM*

Liszt is so known for his piano and orchestral repertoire, most people are unaware that he composed a significant amount of choral music, including five masses and a large number of motets and other small-scale sacred genres. Much of this music was written for the Catholic Church, which fascinated Liszt for most of his life. He even took minor orders and lived in a monastery for two years. Liszt was also drawn to the Cäcilien movement, which had as its mission the return of church music to the ideals of the Council of Trent and the Counter-Reformation. The motets, therefore, as exemplified in *Ave verum,* are a cappella and in clear textures so that the text can be understood easily.

Hail, true body of Christ, born of the Virgin Mary, truly suffered, sacrificed on the cross for mankind, whose side was pierced, whence flowed water and blood, be for us a foretaste when in death we are examined. Amen.

76. ANTON BRUCKNER—*OS JUSTI*

Although much of Bruckner's choral music exemplifies characteristics of the Cäcilien movement, as described above in the commentary on Franz Liszt, Bruckner was not a proponent of the reform precepts; rather, he adhered to the conservative musical characteristics of the geographical area in which he lived and worked most of his life. In addition, much of his sacred music was written not for concert purposes, but for liturgical use in the Augustinian monastery of St. Florian and the cathedral in Linz. This is the case with most of the motets, including *Os justi.* This motet is a cappella, in a texture of alternating sections of homophony and imitative polyphony, and it ends with a statement of Gregorian chant.

The mouth of the righteous will meditate wisdom, and his tongue will speak what is just. The law of his God is in his heart, and his steps will not falter. Alleluia.

77. JOHANNES BRAHMS—*EIN DEUTSCHES REQUIEM* (SELIG SIND, DIE DA LEID TRAGEN)

Brahms composed his Requiem over a period of twelve years, beginning with what is now the fourth movement and ending with the fifth. It may be considered surprising, therefore, that the overall work has many elements of symmetry. As examples: the ending material of movements 1 and 7 are identical; movement 1 is in the tripartite key structure of F-Major / D-flat Major / F-Major, while the seventh movement, as a mirror, is in F-Major / A-Major / F-Major; movements 2 and 6 begin in minor keys, have ABA structures, and close with fugal material; movements 3 and 5 feature soloists; and movement 4, which stands in the middle of the Requiem, has the rondo-like structure of ABACA. The entire Requiem, as represented by the text of movement 1 from Matthew 5:4 and Psalm 126:5–6, consists of selected passages from Martin Luther's translation of the Bible that convey the composer's general view of death as peace after life's many pains.

Blessed are they who bear grief, for they shall be comforted. Those who sow with tears will reap with joy. They go forth and weep and bear precious seeds, and come with joy and bring their sheaves.

78. JOHANNES BRAHMS—*WALDESNACHT, DU WUNDERKÜHLE*

Brahms composed six sets of small-scale secular part songs, beginning with five pieces for male chorus in the early years of his compositional career and ending with five pieces for mixed choir nine years before his death. *Waldesnacht, du wunderkühle* comes from the set composed in 1873 and 1874 entitled *Sieben Lieder*, op. 62. All the pieces in this opus, as well as many of the pieces in the other opuses of part songs, have texts that reflect the tranquil and untroubled state of the countryside and its restorative effects on humankind. Many of the pieces, including *Waldesnacht, du wunderkühle*, are basically homophonic and strophic.

1. *Forest night, so wondrously cool, you a thousand times I greet; after the loud bustle of the world, oh how your rustling is sweet. Dreamily, I sink my tired limbs into the soft shelter of the moss, and I feel as if I would again be rid of all life's insane torments.*
2. *Distant flute song, die away, you that stirs a vast longing and carries thoughts into the beautiful, alas, envied distance. Let the forest night rock me, soothe all pain, and a blessed contentment I will inhale with its fragrances.*

3. *In the secret, narrow circles, you become well, you wild heart, and a peace floats down with soft flutterings. Sing me, lovely bird songs, into a gentle slumber. Insane torments, disappear again, wild heart, now good night.*

79. Joseph Rheinberger—*Abendlied*

Like Bruckner, Rheinberger was not a proponent of the Cäcilien movement, the precepts of which he believed were too limiting and restrictive. However, also like Bruckner, much of Rheinberger's sacred output is modeled on music of the past. This is especially evident in the motets, which are frequently in a neo-Renaissance style. *Abendlied*, for example, is a cappella and in a polyphonic texture. Furthermore, it begins with a dialogue between the upper and lower voices, continues with points of imitation, and ends with a return to the music of the motet's beginning—thus giving the piece an ABA structure. The text is from Luke 24:29.

Remain with us, for it will be evening, and the day will be over.

80. Antonín Dvořák—*V přírodě* (Napadly písně v duši mou)

Dvořák's music is similar in many ways to that of Brahms, who admired Dvořák and promoted his music. The small-scale secular repertoire, for instance, was composed in sets or cycles of opuses, texts are often about pastoral subjects, the organization of musical material often results in repeat structures, and textures are mainly a cappella, homophonic, and strophic. *V přírodě*, which translates as "In nature's realm" or "Songs of nature," is the title given to the complete opus—a collection of five part songs composed in 1882. "Napadly písně v duši mou" is the first piece in the opus and has an ABB structure. The text is from a poem by Vitězslav Hálek.

1. *Songs filled my heart one lovely day, how could I know they would be calling; just like the dew upon the hill, dew never warns us before falling.*
2. *Nature is sparkling heavenly, just as a child is happy, glowing; how can I know if these are songs of joy or merely songs of weeping and woe.*
3. *Now with the moonlight on the dew, gone are the songs that sadden or console me; now as I'm waiting for another dawn, I'm hoping they'll again fill my soul.*

81. Anton Arensky—*Otche nash*

The Divine Liturgy of the Russian Orthodox Church, officially called *Liturgiia Sv. Ioanna Zlatousta* (Liturgy of St. John Chrysostom), consists of numerous traditional texts that, like those in the Roman Catholic Mass, are spoken, chanted, or sung chorally. The Lord's Prayer is common to both Russian and Catholic services. However, it has been set chorally in the Divine Liturgy, while it is traditionally chanted or spoken in the Roman Mass. Arensky's setting, like other notable ones by Nikolai Rimsky-Korsakov and Nicolai Kedroff, is homophonic, without text repetition, and at a soft dynamic level. None of the settings includes the text "for thine is the kingdom, power, and glory forever," which is chanted before the final "Amen."

Our father, who art in heaven, hallowed be thy name, thy kingdom come, thy will be done on earth as it is in heaven. Give us this day our daily bread, and forgive us our debts, as we forgive our debtors, and lead us not into temptation, but deliver us from evil. Amen.

82. ALEKSANDR GRECHANINOV—*SVETE TIHIY*

The text that begins "Svete tihiy" is part of the *Vsenoshchnoye bdeniye* (All-Night Vigil), which is celebrated in the Russian Orthodox Church before major feasts or on Saturday evenings. This service was popular with Russian composers, including Tchaikovsky, Chesnokov, and Rachmaninoff, who wrote complete settings of the Vigil. Most other Russian composers either wrote partial settings or chose a few of the constituent parts and set them as motet-like pieces, and most of the settings of "Svete tihiy," as represented by the one printed here by Grechaninov, are thickly scored and harmonically expansive, with dialogue effects between the upper and lower voices, and with low tessituras for the basses.

Gladsome light of the holy glory of the immortal, heavenly father, holy, blessed, Jesus Christ. Now that we have come to the sun's setting, and behold the light of evening, we praise the father, son, and holy spirit, God. You are worthy at every moment to be praised in hymns by solemn voices, son of God, giver of life, all the world glorifies you.

83. PAVEL CHESNOKOV—*DUH TVOY BLAGIY*

Chesnokov composed a number of sacred pieces that are not a part of either the Divine Liturgy or the All-Night Vigil. Ten of these pieces, which include the composer's most popular repertoire, were written as a cycle of communion hymns published as op. 25. *Duh tvoy blagiy* is the final piece in the cycle and, like many of the other pieces, is formally organized. It has an ABA structure, the A portions featuring short homophonic phrases in dialogue between the upper and lower voices, and the B section composed as an imitative duet between the sopranos and altos. In addition, there is repeat of melodic material in each of the A and B sections. The text is from Psalm 143:10.

Let your good spirit lead me on a level path. Alleluia.

84. SERGE RACHMANINOFF—*VSENOSHCHNOYE BDENIYE* (BOGORODISTE DEVO)

"Bogorodiste devo" is the sixth and most popular of the fifteen pieces or movements in Rachmaninoff's *Vsenoshchnoye bdeniye* (All-Night Vigil), which was composed in a two-week period during January and February of 1915. The work as a whole is based on several forms of Orthodox chant—znamenny (movements 8, 9, 12, 13, and 14), Greek (movements 2 and 15), and Kievan (movements 4 and 5). "Bogorodiste devo," often referred to as "Ave Maria" or "Hail Mary," is one of the six movements not based on chant, although its melodic characteristics are chant-like. The texture of the piece is basically homophonic, with a Russian trademark passage sung by sopranos and tenors in octaves.

Mother of God, rejoice, Mary full of grace, God is with you. Blessed are you among women, and blessed is the fruit of your womb, for you have given birth to the savior of our souls.

85. HUBERT PARRY—*SONGS OF FAREWELL* (MY SOUL, THERE IS A COUNTRY)

Parry contributed significantly to the part song repertoire, composing approximately fifty pieces in the genre and publishing many of them in collections. *My soul, there is a country* is the first piece from his final collection, titled "Songs of Farewell" and composed between 1916 and 1918, the year of his death. The poems for the collection do not deal with the usual pastoral or amorous subjects; instead, they are spiritual in nature and deal mainly with the subject of death and the afterlife. Most of the poems were written by seventeenth-century English poets, including Henry Vaughan (1622–1695), whose poem *Peace* was used for *My soul, there is a country*.

86. CHARLES VILLIERS STANFORD—*BEATI QUORUM VIA*

Stanford's small-scale sacred output includes both English anthems and Latin motets. For the latter genre, Stanford conformed to the prevailing practice of emulating Renaissance styles, scoring pieces for a cappella chorus, and composing them in imitative textures. These traits are evident in the three motets of op. 38—*Justorum animae, Coelos ascendit hodie*, and *Beati quorum via*. The third motet, printed here, features the upper and lower voices in dialogue and a point-of-imitation setting of the words "qui ambulant lege Domini" that word-paints a path from earth to heaven. The text is from Psalm 119:1.

Blessed are the undefiled in the way, who walk in the law of the Lord.

87. EDWARD ELGAR—*AS TORRENTS IN SUMMER*

This part song comes from Elgar's cantata *Scenes from the Saga of King Olaf,* op. 30, the full work scored for soprano, tenor, and bass soloists, chorus, and full orchestra, and premiered at the North Staffordshire Music Festival in 1896. The text for the cantata is an adaptation of the poem *The Saga of King Olaf* by Henry Wadsworth Longfellow (1807–1882), which relates aspects of the life, battles, and death of the Norse crusader. Elgar divides the story into nine scenes, framed by a prologue and an epilogue. "As torrents in summer," which is the only part of the cantata scored for a cappella chorus, is in the epilogue, almost at the end of the cantata. The form of the chorus, following that of the poem, is strophic.

88. LOWELL MASON—*NEARER, MY GOD, TO THEE*

This is one of approximately thirty hymns composed by the American music educator Lowell Mason. It is contained in most Protestant hymnals, usually under the name "Bethany," and was made famous for its alleged performance by the band of the *Titanic* as it sank in the North Atlantic in 1912. The text of the hymn was written in 1841 by the English poet Sarah Flower Adams (1805–1848) and contains five verses—one more than printed with the music here ("Then with my waking thoughts bright with thy praise, out of my stony griefs Bethel I'll raise; so by my woes to be nearer, my God, to thee. . . ."), which occurs as verse 4. Note that Mason's original scoring is in the meter 6/4, not in the common 4/4 seen in most modern printings.

89. EDWARD MACDOWELL—*THE BROOK*

MacDowell, known today for the artist colony he and his wife established in Peterborough, New Hampshire, composed twenty-four part songs. Eighteen are scored for male chorus, three for female chorus, and three others for mixed chorus. Two of those for mixed chorus were published together as *Two Northern Songs,* op. 43, composed between 1890 and 1891 and set to poetry by MacDowell himself. "The brook" is number 1 of the set and is perhaps the best-known American part song of the nineteenth century. It has a strophic quality in that the second half of the piece is similar to the first in melodic and rhythmic design.

90. AMY BEACH—*THREE SHAKESPEARE CHORUSES* (THROUGH THE HOUSE GIVE GLIMMERING LIGHT)

Amy Beach, also known as Mrs. H. H. A. Beach, was mostly known during her day as a concert pianist; she made her performing debut with the Boston Symphony Orchestra when she was seventeen, and during the middle years of her life had an extensive career in Europe. She also was known and admired for her many compositions, which total almost two hundred works and which include eighty-four songs and seventy choral compositions. A large number of the compositions are scored for women's voices; Mrs. Beach, who cofounded and served as the first president of the Society of American Women Composers, was an important advocate of women in music. The *Three Shakespeare Choruses* were composed for and premiered by the Detroit Madrigal Club in 1896. The text is from Shakespeare's *A Midsummer's Night's Dream*, Act 5, Scene 2.

91. CLAUDE DEBUSSY—*TROIS CHANSONS DE CHARLES D'ORLÉANS* (DIEU! QU'IL LA FAIT BON REGARDER)

Debussy's three chansons, set to texts by the Medieval-era French poet Charles d'Orléans (1391–1465), are the composer's only music scored for a cappella chorus. The first and third chansons, "Dieu! qu'il la fait bon regarder" and "Yver, vous n'estes qu'un villain," were composed in 1898 and are similar in structure to the Parisian chansons of the Renaissance, with alternating passages of imitative polyphony and homophony. Both chansons also have an ABA structure. The second chanson, "Quand j'ai ouy le tabourin," was composed in 1908 and is in the style of an accompanied song. The music of all three pieces is characteristic of Debussy's Impressionistic style, with harmonies juxtaposed in nontraditional ways to produce effects of color.

God! she is fair to look upon, graceful, good, and beautiful; for all the great virtues that are hers, everyone is ready to give praise. Who could tire of her? Her beauty is always renewing itself. On neither side of the ocean do I know any woman or girl who is in all virtues so perfect. It is a dream to even think on her: God! she is fair to look upon!

92. MAURICE RAVEL—*TROIS CHANSONS* (NICOLETTE)

Ravel's three chansons, composed in 1914 and 1915, are like those by Debussy in many ways: the first and third pieces are modeled on Parisian chansons of the Renaissance; the second chanson is an accompanied song; and nontraditional harmonies are used to produce effects of color. However, the two composers use different formal structures. "Nicolette," for example, is strophic. Also, Ravel uses modern notational techniques to add color to text expression. Note the nonsense syllables at the end of verse 2, the portamentos in verse 3, and the dissonant minor-second intervals at the beginning of verse 4.

Nicolette, at Vespers time, went walking in the field to pick daisies, daffodils, and lilies of the valley. She jumped merrily in high spirits, looking around here, there, and everywhere. She encountered an old grumbling wolf with bristling fur and glinting eye, who said, "Hey there, Nicolette, do you want to go to grandmother's house?" Breathlessly, Nicolette ran away, losing her cap and white shoes. She then encountered a handsome page with blue trousers and a gray coat, who said, "Hey there, Nicolette, do you want a sweet friend?" Sensibly, poor Nicolette turned away slowly and with a heavy heart. She then encountered an old gray-haired man, crooked and ugly, foul-smelling and fat-bellied, who said, "Hey there, Nicolette, do you want gold?" Quickly, she ran to his arms, and pretty Nicolette never again returned to the fields.

93. FRANK MARTIN—*MASS* (AGNUS DEI)

Martin composed the Kyrie, Gloria, Credo, and Sanctus of his mass for double chorus in 1922 and added the Agnus Dei in 1926. The completed work was not released for performance or publication, however, until 1963, when it was premiered by the Bugenhagen Kantorei of Hamburg. At the time of the premiere Martin wrote: "I considered [the mass to be] between God and myself. I felt then that an expression of religious feelings should remain secret and removed from public opinion." The music, while conservative in terms of harmonic vocabulary and traditional in terms of imitative textures, is not based on models of the past. The Agnus Dei is particularly inventive (and effective): the second chorus chants the text in a steady cortège-like succession of unchanging rhythmic values, while the first chorus sings a melody, mostly in unison, that is frequently in syncopation against the second chorus rhythms. The text is the same as that of #7.

94. ARTHUR HONEGGER—*LE ROI DAVID* (LA MORT DE DAVID)

Honegger's music set to text about the life of King David was composed in 1921 as incidental music to a play, which was staged in its initial performance. Honegger immediately revised the score, however, changing the genre subtitle from "drama biblique" (biblical drama) to "psaume symphonique" (symphonic psalm), reducing the spoken dialogue to short links between musical numbers, and presenting the work in concert form. In this revision, the work was divided into twenty-seven numbers grouped into three parts (David's Youth, David as King, and David's Old Age). "La mort de David" (David's death) is the final movement. The scoring for the revision is for solo voices, chorus, and seventeen wind and percussion instruments, while a further revision in 1923 is for full orchestra, including strings.

The spirit of God speaks through me: A just one will come to men, ruling in the fear of God. He is as the light of the morning, when the sun rises. Oh, this life was so fair! I bless you, you who granted it to me. God says to you: A day will dawn when a flower will blossom from your green stem. And its perfume will fill all the people here below with the breath of life. Hallelujah!

95. LILI BOULANGER—*VIEILLE PRIÈRE BOUDDHIQUE* (PRIÈRE QUOTIDIENNE POUR TOUT L'UNIVERS)

Lili Boulanger, sister of the famous teacher Nadia Boulanger, composed fifteen choral works before her tragic death from cancer at the age of twenty-four. *Vieille prière bouddhique*, one of eight works for chorus and orchestra, was drafted in 1914 and completed in 1917. The text, from the Buddhist *Visuddhimagga*, is subtitled "Prière quotidienne pour tout l'Univers" (Daily prayer for the entire universe). The music, while generally Impressionistic, contains melodic and harmonic elements that are often referred to as exotic and that reflect the Eastern nature of the text.

Let all things that breathe, without enemies, without obstacles, transcending sadness and achieving happiness, be able to move freely along the path that is destined for them. Let all creatures every-where, all spirits and all living things, without enemies. . . . Let all women, let all men, Aryans and non-Aryans, all gods and all humans, and those who have fallen, without enemies. . . . In the East and in the West, the North and the South, that all begins that exist, without enemies. . . .

96. Francis Poulenc—*Quatre motets pour le temps de Noël* (Hodie Christus natus est)

This is one of four motets in a set generally called in English the "Christmas motets." This set, composed in 1951 and 1952, followed a similar collection of four Lenten motets composed in 1938 and 1939. All the motets are a cappella and have Latin texts. *Hodie Christus natus est* reflects Poulenc's general practice of structural organization (repeating large sections of music) and his penchant for stringing together short cubist motifs, all separated by rests. For instance, the first section is comprised of motifs that are in the arrangement aabbcdef, followed by a repeat of the first part of f; the second section is abcdef, followed by a repeat of the second part of f; and the third section is abcdef, followed by several fragments of f. The text is the same as that of #20.

97. Maurice Duruflé—*Requiem* (In Paradisum)

The majority of Duruflé's compositional output is based on Gregorian chant. This includes his *Messe cum jubilo*, four motets, and the *Requiem*, which began as a series of organ pieces based on Gregorian chants. In most instances, Duruflé quotes chant exactly, without elaboration or alteration. In the final movement of the *Requiem*, for example, the choral sopranos begin by singing the "In Paradisum" chant as found in the *Liber usualis*, while the orchestra provides an harmonic accompaniment. For the latter portion of the movement, the chant is given over to the solo organ part while the chorus accompanies homophonically. The entire work exists in a version scored for full orchestra (printed here) and in a scoring by Duruflé himself for organ. The text is an antiphon from the Roman Catholic Requiem Mass.

May angels lead you into Paradise, may the martyrs receive you at your coming and lead you into the holy city of Jerusalem. May a choir of angels receive you, and with the once-poor Lazarus, may you have eternal rest.

98. ARNOLD SCHOENBERG—*VIER STÜCKE,* OP. 27 (UNENTRINNBAR)

Schoenberg composed his *Vier Stücke* (Four Pieces), op. 27, for chorus in 1925, several years after he began writing in the twelve-tone idiom. The first three pieces of the set are a cappella, while the fourth piece is scored for chorus and mandolin, clarinet, violin, and cello. "Unentrinnbar" (Inescapable) is the first piece in the set and is in the form of a strict canon followed by a short homophonic closing. Each statement of the canon consists of the four permutations common to general manipulation of the twelve-tone row, with the soprano and tenor rows in the order of original, retrograde, inversion, and retrograde inversion, and the alto and bass beginning with the inversion. The text, as well as that of the second piece in the set, is by Schoenberg; the texts of the third and fourth pieces are German translations of Chinese poems.

The courageous are those who accomplish acts beyond the measure of their courage. They possess only the strength, the mandate to conceptualize, and the character to refuse rejection. Were a god so ungracious as to grant them a realization of their lot, then they would not be so envied. And that is why they are envied.

99. ANTON WEBERN—*ENTFLIEHT AUF LEICHTEN KÄHNEN*

This is Webern's first choral work, composed in 1908, the same year as his *Passacaglia* for orchestra. Both compositions are based on traditional formal structures (the choral work being a double canon), which undoubtedly reflects Webern's study of older music; he received a doctorate in musicology in 1906. Both works are advanced harmonically, however, and are considered to be atonal. *Entflieht auf leichten Kähnen* was originally scored for a cappella chorus (the version printed here), although Webern added an accompaniment of violin, viola, cello, harmonium, and piano in 1914. The text is from the poem *Das Jahr der Seele* by Stefan George (1868–1933), one of Webern's favorite poets, and the structure of the music in three sections reflects the poem's three verses.

Flee in light boats from intoxicated worlds of sun that milder tears might always reward you for your flight. Watch this frenzy of blond, light blue visions and drunken delights unfold, devoid of ecstasy. That the sweet shudders in the new suffering will not envelop you—let it be the silent sorrow that fills this spring.

100. PAUL HINDEMITH—*SIX CHANSONS* (LA BICHE)

Hindemith composed his set of six chansons in 1938 for the Swiss conductor and composer Georges Haenni (1896–1980) and his choral ensemble Chanson Valaisanne. Hindemith had

976 Notes and Translations

just moved from Germany to Switzerland and was attracted to Valais, in the southwestern area of the country. The music represents the composer's style of "Gebrauchsmusik" (functional or practical music) in that its demands, in terms of pitch and rhythm, are not great. The music also represents Hindemith's tonal style, referred to as "pandiatonic" (indicating the use of the chromatic scale in a diatonic manner). In "En hiver," the fifth chanson in the set, Hindemith employs all but two notes of the chromatic scale while maintaining a tonic sense of E-flat Major. The chansons are all also structured with repeat patterns. "La Biche," for example, is basically in an ABCA form. The texts are all by Rainer Maria Rilke (1875–1926), a German poet who wrote approximately four hundred poems in French.

O doe, what lovely ancient forest depths abound in your eyes; how much open trust mixed with how much fear. All this, borne by the lively gracility of your bounds. But nothing ever disturbs that unpossessive unawareness of your brow.

101. HUGO DISTLER—*LOBE DEN HERREN,* OP. 6/I, NO. 2

Much of Distler's music, including the motet here, is composed in a style that emulates the German Lutheran music of the late Renaissance, especially the music of Heinrich Schütz. During Distler's student days in Leipzig he became interested in the historic music sung by the Thomanerchor, and during his time working in various churches and schools he became involved in several movements that sought to return the Lutheran Church (liturgy, music, and organ building) to older, original principles. In terms of composition, Distler often set chorale tunes such as "Lobe den Herren" here, which was written (text and music) by Joachim Neander (1650–1680), who was one of the most important Lutheran hymnists of the seventeenth century. In addition, Distler often composed sets of music for the liturgical year, giving the sets titles used by Schütz and other early composers. For example, Distler's op. 12 from 1934 to 1936 is titled *Geistliche Chormusik,* and his op. 6/I from 1933 is titled *Kleine Geistliche Abendmusik.* "Lobe den Herren" is the second of three motets in op. 6/I. Of the five verses of the original chorale, Distler set the first two, arranging them in an ABA format.

1. *Praise the Lord, the mighty king of glory, my dear soul, that is what I desire. Come to the assembly, psalter and harp awake, let the music be heard.*
2. *Praise the Lord, who splendidly rules over everything, who has led you on eagle's wings, who supports you and has given you pleasure. Have you not perceived this?*

102. PABLO CASALS—*O VOS OMNES*

Casals composed in a conservative style, one that reflected his interest in the standard nineteenth-century cello repertoire he played in recitals across Europe, Russia, South America, and the United States. Most of his choral works are Latin motets, characterized by traditional functional harmonies, rhythms that reflect a natural declamation of text, and uncomplicated textures. *O vos omnes* is basically homophonic, with phrases of text clearly delineated, and with the motet's opening melodic material used as a closing. The piece, therefore, has an ABCA structure. The text is from the Roman Catholic antiphon for the third Nocturn of Holy Saturday.

O all ye who pass by the way, attend and see if there is any sorrow like my sorrow.

103. Luigi Dallapiccola—*Sei cori di Michelangelo Buonarroti il giovane* (Il coro delle malmaritate)

This is the first of six secular pieces composed between 1933 and 1936 to poetry of Michelangelo Buonarotti the Younger (1568–1646), nephew of the famous sculptor and painter of the Sistine Chapel ceiling. The texts reflect characteristics of Petrarch (1304–1374), whose poems were used frequently by early-Renaissance Italian madrigalists, and likewise, Dallapiccola's music reflects characteristics of the early madrigals. For instance, the first two pieces in the set, "Il coro delle malmaritate" (Chorus of the unhappy wives) and "Il coro dei malammogliati" (Chorus of the unhappy husbands), have alternating passages of homophony and imitative polyphony and also varied rhythms for expressive effect.

From our misfortune, young maids, learn this lesson, from our misfortune, this lesson, young maids, and you'll not say with bitter weeping: Wretched, unhappy women! Better for us most surely! Shut in a little convent, to have lopped off our tresses, renouncing names and adornments, dressed in black, gray, or white, to castigate our bodies with cords of rope and scourges for to better ourselves! Better for us most surely to rise and go to matins, with little trembling tapers, long ere the cock crows. To hide in a Bigallo, enroll in a Rosano, end up in a Majano, at Portico, Bolderone, give up all, in Mugnone take on a veil at Lapo's, or else to hide our head in a Monticel di buoi. Better for us most surely! Learn then this lesson and make sure that you think, think, think, be sure, or else they'll titter and greet you with: Heigh ho, heigh ho.

104. Béla Bartók—*Štyri slovenské piesne* (Na holi)

Like a number of composers in the early part of the twentieth century, including fellow Hungarian Zoltán Kodály (1882–1967), Bartók was interested in native folk material. He collected thousands of folk songs and published nine volumes of arrangements for two- and three-part children's chorus and approximately twenty-five arrangements for mixed chorus. *Štyri slovenské piesne* (Four Slovak Folk Songs), published around 1916 and scored with piano accompaniment, is his most popular set. The piece printed here is titled *Szénagyüjtéskor énekelt dal* (Song of the Hay-Harvesters from Hiadei) and is, characteristically, in extended and mixed meters. It is also strophic (choral parts only).

Where the Alps freely soar, with flowers in the valleys, I rest softly. My work is done for the day and the barn filled with hay. It is night and we can return home peacefully.

105. Zoltán Kodály—*Missa brevis* (Kyrie)

Although known today as a music educator who developed a system of sight-reading based on solfège syllables and also as a musicologist who collected and transcribed thousands of folk songs, Kódaly composed a number of significant sacred choral works. The *Missa brevis*, originally composed as an organ mass, was transcribed for chorus in 1948. It contains all five portions of the Roman Catholic Mass Ordinary plus opening and closing instrumental movements entitled, respectively, "Introitus" and "Ite, missa est." The music is characterized by modal harmonies and imitative textures that reflect Kodály's devotion to Hungarian music of past centuries. The text is the same as that of #3.

106. Krzysztof Penderecki—*Passio et mors domini nostri Jesu Christi secundum Lucam* (Final Scene)

Penderecki's *St. Luke Passion*, as it is generally called, was commissioned by the West German Radio to commemorate, in 1966, the seven hundredth anniversary of the founding of Münster Cathedral. It is modeled on the passions of J. S. Bach, with a division of the work in two movements and with reflective texts interspersed between the biblical passages. In addition, Penderecki paid homage to Bach by using his name as a musical motif (B-flat ["B" in German nomenclature], A, C, and B-natural ["H" in German nomenclature]) more than one hundred times throughout the score, including several times—both in its original and inverted formats—in the final scene. The general fabric of the music is avant-garde, with newly created notational symbols, aleatoric passages, quarter tones, and sprechstimme. The text of the final scene is from Luke 23:44–46, John 19:30, and Psalm 31:1–3, 5.

It was about the sixth hour, and there was darkness over all the earth until the ninth hour. And the sun was darkened, and the veil of the temple was rent in the midst. And Jesus cried with a loud voice: Father, into your hands I commend my spirit. And having said this, he died. It is finished. In thee, Lord, I trust, let me never be confounded; deliver me in your righteousness. Incline your ear to me, deliver me speedily, be my strong protector and a house of defense, to save me. Into your hand I commend my spirit, you have redeemed me, Lord God of truth.

107. IGOR STRAVINSKY—*MASS* (GLORIA)

Stravinsky composed his *Mass* between 1944 and 1947, during his so-called neoclassical period, when his writing was characterized by traditional formal structures, sparse textures, scoring focused on wind instruments, and a harmonic language based on functional tonality. The *Mass*, for example, is in an arch form: the Kyrie and Agnus Dei movements are entirely choral, basically homophonic, and in three sections; the Gloria and Sanctus movements feature soloists and are melismatic; and the Credo stands alone as, in the composer's words, "a statement of faith." In addition, the scoring of the *Mass* is for double woodwind quintet (two oboes, English horn, two bassoons, two trumpets, and three trombones). Apart from these characteristics, the Gloria and Credo illustrate Stravinsky's penchant for repetition of rhythmic patterns in a motoristic manner.

Glory to God in the highest, and on earth peace to men of goodwill. We praise you, we bless you, we worship you, we glorify you. We give thanks to you according to your great glory. Lord God, king of heaven, God the father almighty. Lord Jesus Christ, the only begotten son, Lord God, lamb of God, son of the father. Who takes away the sins of the world, have mercy on us. Who takes away the sins of the world, receive our prayer. Who sits at the right hand of the father, have mercy on us. For you alone are holy, you alone are Lord, you alone are most high, Jesus Christ, with the holy spirit in the glory of God the father. Amen.

108. SERGEY PROKOFIEV—*ALEKSANDR NEVSKY* (ALEKSANDR'S ENTRY INTO PSKOV)

This cantata-like work was composed during a period of time when Prokofiev was focusing on the composition of music for children (e.g., *Peter and the Wolf*) and on music set to patriotic texts. *Aleksandr Nevsky* (Alexander Nevsky), op. 78, was originally composed in 1938 as music for the film by Sergei Eisenstein about Nevsky's defeat of Teutonic invaders at the Battle on the Ice at Lake Chudskoye in 1242. The film and its music were so successful, Prokofiev took parts of the film score and fashioned them in 1939 into a separate work divided into seven movements—Russia under the Mongolian Yoke; Song about Alexander Nevsky; The Crusaders in Pskov.; Arise, ye Russian People; The Battle on the Ice; The Field of the Dead; and Alexander's Entry into Pskov. The work as a whole is richly scored, with numerous percussion instruments (including bells, glockenspiel, xylophone, and tambourine), and the melodic content of many of the movements, especially the last, has elements of Russian folk songs.

Russia marched to mighty battle; Russia overcame the enemy; on our native soil let no foe exist. Whoever invades will be killed. Be merry, sing, mother of Russia! In our native Russia, let no foe exist, let no foe see our native villages. Whoever invades Russia will be killed. In our native Russia, in great Russia let no foe exist. At the mighty festival all Russia has gathered together. Be merry, Russia, our mother!

109. Veljo Tormis—*Laulusild*

Tormis is one of a number of modern-day Estonian composers who are devoted to the folk material of their country. Like Bartók and Kodály in the early years of the twentieth century, Tormis is a collector of folk melodies and a composer who incorporates these melodies into his original compositions. He is particularly known for his settings of "regisvärsid," or ancient runic folk songs. He is also known for combining folk material from different Baltic countries. *Laulusild* (Bridge of Song), for example, includes both Finnish and Estonian folk songs (first separately and then together). The text is from an Estonian folk song and the *Kalevala*, the Finnish epic folk poem about the ancient lands called Kaleva. The structure of *Laulusild* is strophic, with two major verses, the first of which is further divided into repeated phrases.

I have a good mind to take into my head and begin singing, begin reciting, reeling off a tale of kin, singing a tale of their kind. The words unfreeze in my mouth, the phrases tumble, they scramble on my tongue, scatter on my teeth. When I start to sing, alleaa, to spin a yarn, alleaa. Dear brother, little brother, fair one who grew up with me. Begin singing with me, begin reciting with me since we are now together, since we have come from two ways; we seldom get together, meet each other, on these poor borders, the luckless lands of the north. Let us strike hand to hand, fingers into finger snaps, sing of good things, bring forth some of the best things, for those dear ones to hear, for those with a mind to know, among the young ones rising, among the people growing.

110. Arvo Pärt—*Berliner Messe* (Kyrie)

The *Berliner Messe* was originally composed in 1990 for the German Catholic Days celebrated in Berlin and scored for SATB soloists and organ. Pärt rescored it in 1991 for SATB chorus and strings, and in 1997 he made an arrangement of the string accompaniment for organ. The mass is comprised of the traditional five portions of the Latin Ordinary plus two Alleluia verses—"Emitte spiritum tuum" (Send forth your spirit) and "Veni sancte spiritus reple tuorum corda fidelium" (Come holy spirit, fill the hearts of your faithful people)—and the motet "Veni sancte spiritus, et emitte coelitus lucis tuae radium" (Come, holy spirit, and send forth a ray of your heavenly light). The music, typical of Pärt's writing after 1976, is in a minimalistic style characterized by the blending of diatonic scales and triadic arpeggios, called by Pärt "tintinnabuli" (from the effect of sound lingering after a bell has been struck). The text is the same as that of #3, 6, and 16.

111. Jean Sibelius—*Finlandia*

Like many composers of his generation, Sibelius was interested in folk material of his native country; he studied its history, collected folk songs, and composed music (e.g., *Kullervo*) that paid homage to the past. Sibelius was also interested in the current state of his country and wrote a number of works that were political in nature and that served to promote Finnish independence from Russia. These works include *Atenarnes sång* (Song of the Athenians), *Isånmaalle* (To the Fatherland), and his most famous work, *Suomi herää* (Finland Awakens), which was later renamed *Finlandia*. This last work was originally composed in 1899 as an orchestral tone poem for a political rally in support of free speech. In 1927 Sibelius extracted the final portion of the work and published it as the last section of his Masonic Ritual Music, op. 113, with text by the opera singer Väinö Sola. A decade later he replaced those words with others by the popular Finnish poet and essayist Veikko Antero Koskenniemi (1886–1962), the opening phrase of which is, "Oi, Suomi, katso, sinum päiväs koittaa" (O Finland, look, your dawn approaches). This text subsequently became famous around the world as a hymn and as the popular, although not official, national anthem of Finland. The text of the hymn printed in many twentieth- and twenty-first-century Protestant hymnals begins "Be still, my soul, the Lord is on thy side."

112. EINOJUHANI RAUTAVAARA—*SUITE DE LORCA* (CANCIÓN DE JINETE)

Although Rautavaara studied in Finland and received a degree in musicology, his interests have been beyond those of his native country, and for much of his choral music he has chosen poetry by major European writers of the early twentieth century. *Suite de Lorca*, for example, employs four poems by Federico García Lorca (1898–1936)—"Canción de jinete" (The Rider's Song), "El grito" (The Scream), "La luna asoma" (The Moon Comes Out), and "Malagueña." The music is basically tonal, with rhythmic characteristics of Spanish popular songs, and each of the four pieces has a different textural or harmonic feature—ostinatos in "Canción de jinete," glissandos in "El grito," a Phrygian scale in "La luna asoma," and guitar-like effects in "Malagueña."

Córdoba, far away and alone. Small black horse, large moon, and olives in my saddle bags. Although I may know the roads, I never will arrive in Córdoba. Through the plains, through the wind, small black horse, red moon. Death is looking at me from the towers of Córdoba. Oh, that road is so long! Oh, my valiant pony! Oh, that death awaits me, before arriving in Córdoba! Córdoba, far away and alone.

113. PER NØRGÅRD—*I HEAR THE RAIN*

Much of Nørgård's choral music reflects his cosmopolitan training (he studied in his native Denmark as well as in France and Germany) and his exposure to the avant-garde music of Karlheinz Stockhausen, Pierre Boulez, and Luciano Berio. Nørgård's music is also highly expressive and reflective of natural occurrences in nature and in life. *Jeg hører regnen* (I hear the rain), for example, was inspired by the sounds of the ocean and the overtones the waves seem to produce. The music begins with whispered and sibilant sounds, with changing vowels performed independently by the singers, and also the aleatoric execution of finger snaps, claves, or drums. During the remainder of the piece, the sopranos, altos, and basses are scored in a melodically tonal texture, while the tenor part is punctuated by the terse recitation of a few words. The text is by the Danish poet Michael Strunge (1958–1986), with English translation (the only text printed in the published score) by Nørgård.

114. Ralph Vaughan Williams—*Five English Folk Songs* (The dark-eyed sailor)

During the early years of the twentieth century, Vaughn Williams, along with his compatriot Gustav Holst, traveled the British Isles and collected more than eight hundred folk melodies. Vaughan Williams then made choral arrangements of approximately thirty of these melodies. The set of *Five English Folksongs* was composed in 1913 and includes "The dark-eyed sailor," "The spring time of the year," "Just as the tide was flowing," "The lover's ghost," and "Wassail Song." Each of these pieces is a free arrangement of the original tune, with the melody changing voice parts in the different strophes of text and with added supplementary musical material. In "The dark-eyed sailor," for example, the five verses of text move among the voice parts in order to exemplify the narrative character of the story being portrayed.

115. Gustav Holst—*Lullay my liking*

While Holst had a strong interest in folksongs of the British Isles (collecting hundreds of them with Vaughan Williams) and also interest in Hindu literature and philosophy (composing four groups of hymns from the Rig Veda), he is best remembered for his orchestral work *The Planets* and for his several choral settings of Christmas texts. Most popular of these Christmas pieces are the carols *In the bleak midwinter*, set to a poem by Christina Rossetti (1830–1894), and *Lullay my liking*, set to an anonymous English poem of the Medieval era. Both carols are strophic. However, *Lullay my liking* is unique in that the verses are set as unison solo lines followed by a choral refrain. In addition, the meters of the verses and refrain are varied to provide a sense of natural declamation.

116. Herbert Howells—*Like as the Hart Desireth the Waterbrooks*

The anthem and related Anglican liturgical works were important during the twentieth century, especially in England, where virtually all the composers of the period made significant contributions to the genres. Howells, for example, composed more than one hundred anthems, motets, canticles, and hymns. Of these, his Christmas carol *A spotless rose* and his anthem *Like as the hart desireth the waterbrooks* are most popular. This latter piece was composed in 1941 as part of a set of four anthems (another being *O pray for the peace of Jerusalem*), and is scored over-all for SATB chorus and organ, although most of the anthem is for unison and two-part chorus. The appealing musical style, with lushly scored harmonies, is an exemplar of the anthem in England during the early years of the Modern era.

117. WILLIAM WALTON—*SET ME AS A SEAL UPON THINE HEART*

Compared to other major British composers of his generation, Walton's choral output is small, consisting of only twenty works. However, many of these works are well-known and highly acclaimed, including his oratorio *Belshazzar's Feast*, his motet *Where does the uttered music go*, and his wedding anthem *Set me as a seal upon thine heart*. This anthem was composed for the wedding of Ivor Wimborne and Mabel Fox-Stangways on St. Cecilia's Day (St. Cecilia being the patron saint of music), November 22, 1938. The music is in ABA form, with a tenor soloist beginning the first three phrases of the initial A section and a soprano soloist singing a phrase in the final A section. The text is adapted from the Song of Solomon 8:6–7.

118. MICHAEL TIPPETT—*A CHILD OF OUR TIME* (DEEP RIVER)

The first of Tippett's three oratorios, *A Child of Our Time* was composed in 1938 in reaction to the "Kristallnacht," the harassment and murder of Jews and destruction of their property throughout Germany and Austria on November 9 and 10 of that year. The oratorio also reflects the composer's study of Jungian psychology, with particular emphasis on elements of light and darkness; the motto "The darkness declares the glory of light" is at the head of the oratorio. The music, which according to Tippett is "direct and simple," is divided into three parts, each further divided into multiple, connected movements. The content and arrangement of the movements are based on the Passions of J. S. Bach, with recitatives, arias, choruses, and chorales. For the chorales, which are reflective commentaries, Tippett chose five African American spirituals, the final of which, and the one that closes the oratorio, is "Deep River." The oratorio was first performed by the Morley College choirs and the London Philharmonic Orchestra in March 1944.

119. BENJAMIN BRITTEN—*A CEREMONY OF CAROLS* (WOLCUM YOLE)

Britten's choral output is extensive and diverse, from large-scale choral/orchestral works such as the *War Requiem* to sets of a cappella part songs such as the *Five Flower Songs*. There is little that unifies all the repertoire, although Britten wrote frequently for treble voices. Examples include the cantata *Saint Nicolas*, the *Missa Brevis*, the choral variations *A Boy Was Born*, and *A Ceremony of Carols*, which is a setting of nine Medieval and Renaissance Christmas poems framed by the Gregorian chant *Hodie Christus natus est* (Today Christ is born). The music of *A Ceremony of Carols*, composed in 1942 during a voyage from the United States to England, is characterized by canonic and echo effects and colorful harp sonorities. "Wolcum Yole" is the first piece in the set following the opening chant.

120. THEA MUSGRAVE—*ON THE UNDERGROUND* SET I (BENEDICTION)

Beginning in 1986, the London subway system (called the "Underground"), as part of a public arts program, began posting poems in the cars alongside the advertisements. The project became so popular, a number of the poems were published in anthologies entitled *Poems on the Underground*. Musgrave took an interest in the project and in 1994 made a cappella settings of random poems, which she combined into three sets, each given a separate subtitle—Set I, "On gratitude, love, and madness"; Set II, "The Strange and the Exotic"; and Set III, "A Medieval Summer." The first piece in Set I, "Benediction," is to the poem of the same name by Jamaican-born poet James Berry (b. 1924). The music is in an advanced tonal idiom, unified by a rising scalar passage set to the word "Thanks."

121. JOHN TAVENER—*HYMN TO THE MOTHER OF GOD*

Most of Tavener's choral works, especially those after the late 1970s, are a cappella settings of texts from or related to Greek Orthodox liturgies. This is the case with his popular *Song for Athene*, which was commissioned by the BBC in 1994 and made famous by its performance at the funeral service of Princess Diana in Westminster Abbey on September 6, 1997. Also of Greek Orthodox derivation is the "Hymn to the Mother of God," which is the first piece from a set entitled *Two Hymns to the Mother of God* (the other piece is "Hymn for the Dormition of the Mother of God"). Both pieces feature Tavener's recognizable textures of block chords with static rhythms. The harmonies in "Hymn to the Mother of God" are especially interesting in that the two choruses cadence at different points.

122. CHARLES IVES—*THREE HARVEST HOME CHORALES* (HARVEST HOME #1)

The set of *Three Harvest Home Chorales*, composed around 1902 and revised a decade later, represents Ives as a nontraditional and experimental composer—juxtaposing meters unconventionally, employing unusual harmonies that often result in striking dissonances, and notating rhythms in new and creative manners. For example, three different meters occur simultaneously in the second of the three chorales (4/4 per measure in the soprano and alto parts, 3/2 per measure in the tenor part, and 9/2 over the space of two measures in the bass part), chord clusters set as choral recitative occur in "Harvest Home #1," and a glissando is notated in "Harvest Home #2." Furthermore, melodic inversion of phrases is employed in "Harvest Home #1." The texts for the chorales are by three relatively unknown preachers— George Burges, John Hampton Gurney, and Henry Alford.

123. RANDALL THOMPSON—*THE PEACEABLE KINGDOM* (THE PAPER REEDS BY THE BROOKS)

Thompson is best known for his so-called Americana choral works. These include the a cappella *Alleluia*, which was commissioned for the 1940 opening of the Boston Symphony Orchestra Berkshire Music Center at Tanglewood; *Frostiana*, a collection of seven settings in various voicings of poems by Robert Frost; and *The Peaceable Kingdom*, a setting of numerous passages from Isaiah divided into eight movements and inspired by one of the "Peaceable Kingdom" paintings by Edward Hicks (1780–1849). As a subtitle to and explanation of the music and painting, Thompson quotes Isaiah 11:6–9, which begins, "The wolf also shall dwell with the lamb, and the leopard shall lie down with the kid." The fifth movement of the work, "The paper reeds by the brooks," is in two musically similar sections, with Thompson's inimitable harmonic language of diatonic melodies in parallel motion chords.

124. VINCENT PERSICHETTI—*FLOWER SONGS* (SPOUTING VIOLETS)

Of Persichetti's twenty choral works, six are settings of poetry by e. e. cummings (1894–1962), who wrote almost three thousand poems, most of them notable for their use of lowercase letters and unusual syntactic arrangements. The collection of *Flower Songs*, commissioned by the Philadelphia Singers and premiered by them in 1984, contains seven settings, the second of which is titled by Persichetti "Spouting Violets," although the original poem is called "the sky was candy luminous." The music is characterized by the composer's penchant for an accessible pandiatonic harmonic idiom.

125. DANIEL PINKHAM—*FOUR ELEGIES* (AT THE ROUND EARTH'S IMAGIN'D CORNERS)

One of the most prolific composers of choral music in the twentieth century, Pinkham wrote more than two hundred works ranging from large-scale choral/orchestral oratorios to short a cappella anthems and part songs. His musical style is also diverse in that many of the shorter works are tonal and rhythmically uncomplicated, while other works are tonally dissonant and rhythmically complex. Most of the repertoire, however, is in a pantonal idiom with carefully notated rhythms that emulate natural speech declamation. This is the case with the *Four Elegies*, composed in 1979 and scored for tenor solo, SATB chorus, chamber orchestra (English horn, French horn, bassoon, organ, and strings), and electronic tape. Texts are by the sixteenth- and seventeenth-century British poets Robert Herrick ("To his dying brother, Master William Herrick"), Richard Crashaw ("Upon the death of a friend"), Henry Vaughan ("Silence, and stealth of days"), and John Donne ("At the round earth's imagin'd corners").

126. NED ROREM—*FOUR MADRIGALS* (LOVE)

The majority of Rorem's choral output is similar in scope and style to his many solo art songs, of which he has composed more than four hundred. The choral repertoire is generally small-scale in both length and scoring, the melodies are often lyrical in quality, and the rhythms are generally straightforward and compatible to the declamation of the texts being set. The *Four Madrigals* of 1947 exhibit all these traits. In addition, they are noteworthy examples of the trend by twentieth-century composers to pay homage to the historical precedents of genres by emulating qualities of their texture and structure. For example, Rorem's madrigals are in a neo-Renaissance style, with alternating passages of homophony and imitative polyphony. The texts of the madrigals are English translations of poetry by the ancient Greek poet Sappho. "Love" is the third madrigal in the set.

127. DOMINICK ARGENTO—*PETER QUINCE AT THE CLAVIER* (MOVEMENT IV)

During the 1980s Argento focused his choral output on cantata-like works set to long and profound poems. These include *Peter Quince at the Clavier* (1980), set to the poem of the same name by the American poet Wallace Stevens (1879–1955); *I Hate and I Love* (1982), set to poetry by the ancient Roman poet Gaius Valerius Catullus (c. 84 BCE–c. 54 BCE), and *A Tocatta of Galuppi's* (1989), set to poetry by the British Victorian poet Robert Browning (1812–1889). In a commentary about *Peter Quince at the Clavier*, Argento writes, "Stevens' poem takes [the story of Susanna and the Elders from an apocryphal chapter in the Book of Daniel] for a metaphor of the emotive power of beauty on the human spirit (in particular, the beauty of music), its use and abuse in stirring our feelings, and its lingering strength in memory." The fourth, and final, movement of the work encapsulates the message of beauty through music.

128. Morten Lauridsen—*Madrigali* (Amor, io sento l'alma)

Lauridsen began his compositional career with four choral works that have become staples of programming with ensembles throughout the world. These include the *Mid-Winter Songs* of 1980, the *Madrigali* of 1987, *Les Chansons des Roses* in 1993, and *O Magnum Mysterium* in 1994. The set of *Madrigali*, subtitled "Six 'Fire Songs' on Italian Renaissance Poems," was inspired by the madrigals of Monteverdi and Gesualdo and set to texts used by these composers and other late-Renaissance madrigalists. According to Lauridsen, "Italian love poems of [the Renaissance] have constituted a rich lyric source for many composers, and while reading them I became increasingly intrigued by the symbolic image of flames, burning, and fire that recurred within this context." The musical textures are replete with Renaissance techniques, including word painting and eye music (e.g., the phrase "Luci serene e chiare" begins with two whole notes that depict "eyes serene and clear"), and the harmonies are unified by what the composer terms the "fire chord" (a minor triad with an added major second). "Amor, io sento l'alma," the fourth madrigal in the set, is composed to a poem by Jhan Gero, who flourished between 1540 and 1555.

Love, I feel my soul return to the fire where I rejoiced and more than ever desire to burn. I burn and in bright flames I feed my miserable heart; the more it is in flames, the more my loving grows, for all my sorrows are born from the fire where I rejoiced and more than ever desire to burn.

129. Eric Whitacre—*Water Night*

Whitacre developed a unique and effective compositional style early in his career. While an undergraduate student in his twenties he composed several works that feature pandiatonic chord clusters used with repeated melodic phrases to create an organic and forward-moving structure. Examples include *Go, lovely rose* of 1990, *Cloudbust* of 1992, and *Water Night* of 1995. He also developed a sensitivity for the keys of his compositions, with scorings of *Water Night* in B-flat Minor and *Lux Aurumque* (composed in 2000) in C-sharp Minor that seem to make the keys inextricably bound to the music. The structure of *Water Night* can be seen as ABA in that the opening material returns at the end of the piece, and the clusters create chords of up to fourteen notes. The text is an English translation of a poem by Octavio Paz (1914–1998).

GENRES

ANTHEM

BALLETTO AND BALLETT

CANTATA

CANZONET

CAROL

CHANSON

CHANT

CHORALE

FOLK SONG SETTING

HYMN

LIED

LUTE SONG

MADRIGAL

MAGNIFICAT

MASS

MOTET

26. Orlando di Lasso—*Musica Dei donum optimi*

28. Jacob Handl—*Pater noster*

29. Hans Leo Hassler—*Dixit Maria*

31. Melchior Franck—*Meine Schwester, liebe Braut*

33. William Byrd—*Ave verum corpus*

47. Michel-Richard de Lalande—*Super flumina Babylonis* (Hymnum cantate nobis)

49. Samuel Scheidt—*Angelus ad pastores*, SSWV13

51. Johann Ludwig Bach—*Das ist meine Freude*

55. John Blow—*Salvator mundi*

59. Juan Gutiérrez de Padilla—*Versa est in luctum*

60. Ignacio Jerusalem—*Responsorio sequndo de Santa José*

62. Michael Haydn—*Salve regina*, MH634

75. Franz Liszt—*Ave verum*

76. Anton Bruckner—*Os justi*

79. Joseph Rheinberger—*Abendlied*

86. Charles Villiers Stanford—*Beati quorum via*

96. Francis Poulenc—*Quatre motets pour le temps de Noël* (Hodie Christus natus est)

101. Hugo Distler—*Lobe den Herren*, op. 6/I, no. 2

102. Pablo Casals—*O vos omnes*

ORATORIO

42. Giacomo Carissimi—*Jonas* (Peccavimus Domine)

57. George Frideric Handel—*Saul* (How excellent thy name, O Lord)

61. Joseph Haydn—*The Creation* (Achieved is the glorious work)

68. Hector Berlioz—*La damnation de Faust* (Apothéose de Marguerite)

73. Felix Mendelssohn—*Elias* (Siehe, der Hüter Israels) / *Elijah* (He, watching over Israel)

94. Arthur Honegger—*Le roi David* (La mort de David)

118. Michael Tippett—*A Child of Our Time* (Deep River)

PART SONG

64. Franz Schubert—*Die Nacht*

69. Camille Saint-Saëns—*Calme des nuits*

74. Robert Schumann—*Minnespiel*, op. 101 (So wahr die Sonne scheinet)

78. Johannes Brahms—*Waldesnacht, du wunderkühle*

80. Antonín Dvořák –*V přírodě* (Napadly písně v duši mou)

85. Hubert Parry—*Songs of Farewell* (My soul, there is a country)

87. Edward Elgar—*As torrents in summer*

89. Edward MacDowell—*The brook*

PASSION

PASTORALE

PSALM SETTING

REQUIEM

Russian Orthodox Motet

81. Anton Arensky—*Otche nash*
82. Aleksandr Grechaninov—*Svete tihiy*
83. Pavel Chesnokov—*Duh tvoy blagiy*
84. Serge Rachmaninoff—*Vsenoshchnoye bdeniye* (Bogoroditse devo)

Villancico

23. Francisco Guerrero—*A un niño llorando*

Villanella

27. Orlando di Lasso—*Tutto lo dì*

Sources and Permissions

1. *Liber usualis*, edited by the Benedictines of Solesmes, 1953, republished 1997. Vertical episemas, which were editorial additions in the *Liber usualis* not found in the original chant manuscript, have been removed.
2. *Wiesbaden Codex.*
3. *Guillaume de Machaut: Oeuvres complètes.*
4. *Johannes Ciconia*, ed. S. Clercx.
5. Bologna, Bibl. Univ. MS 2216.
6. *Guillaume Dufay, Missa L'arme (Kyrie), CMM 1–3, pp. 33–36.* © 1962 American Institute of Musicology. Reproduced with permission.
7. *Werken van Josquin Des Prés.*
8. *Clément Janequin: Chansons polyphoniques*, ed. A. T. Merritt and F. Lesure.
9. *Anthologie Chorale* from *Maîtres Musiciens de la Renaissance Française.*
10. *Claude Le Jeune Airs (1608).*
11. *Jan Pieterszoon Sweelinck Opera omnia.*
12. *Second Book of Madrigals (1538).*
13. *Jacques Arcadelt, Io dico, che fra voi, CMM 31–2, pp. 49-50.* © 1970 American Institute of Musicology. Reproduced with permission.
14. *Cipriano de Rore, Ancor che col partire, CMM 14–4, pp. 31–33.* © 1969 American Institute of Musicology. Reproduced with permission.
15. *Motettorum liber secundus (1572).*
16. *G. P. da Palestrina: Le opera complete.*
17. *Canzonette libro quarto (1590).*
18. *Il quinto libro de madrigale (1591).*
19. *Balletti, 5vv, con li suoi versi per cantare, sonare, & ballare. . . (1591)*
20. *Giovanni Gabrieli, Hodie Christus natus est, CMM 12-9, pp. 173–181.* © 1996 American Institute of Musicology. Reproduced with permission.
21. *Madrigale libro sesto (1611).*
22. *C. de Morales: Opera omnia*, ed. H. Anglès.
23. *Canciones y villanescas espirituales (1589).*
24. *Motecta (1572).*
25. *Heinrich Isaac: Opera omnia.*
26. *Orlando di Lasso sämtlicher Werke, neue Reihe.*
27. *Orlando di Lasso sämtlicher Werke, neue Reihe.*
28. *Tomus Primus Operis musici cantionum (1586).*
29. *Cantiones sacrae (1597).*
30. *Michael Praetorius musikalische Werke.*
31. *Geistliche Gesäng und Melodeyen (1608).*
32. *Mornying and Evenyng prayer and Communion*, published by John Day (1565).
33. *Gradualia ac cantiones sacrae. . . liber primus (1610).*
34. *The First Booke of Balletts to Five Voyces*, published by Thomas Este (1595).
35. *The Firste Booke of Songs or Ayers. . . with Tableture for the Lute (1597).*
36. *Musica Deo sacra et ecclesiae anglicanae (1668).*

37. *The First Set of English Madrigales*, published by Thomas Este (1598).

38. *Thomas Weelkes: Collected Anthems.*

39. *First Book of Selected Church Musick*, printed by John Barnard (1641).

40. *Selva morale e spiritual* (1641).

41. *Il quarto libro de madrigale* (1603).

42. *Giacomo Carissimi: Le opera complete.*

43. *Messa di S Cecilia* (1720).

44. *Dresden Mus. 2159/D/5.*

45. *Istitulo Italiano Antonio Vivaldi.*

46. Marc-Antoine Charpentier, *Mélanges autographes.*

47. *Motets de M. Delalande.*

48. *Heinrich Schütz Neue Ausgabe sämtliche Werke.*

49. *Cantiones sacrae* (1620).

50. *Dietrich Buxtehude: Werke*

51. From the Library of Princess Anna Amalia of Prussia, housed in the Staatsbibliothek, Berlin, and *Das Chorwerk* (1964).

52. *Georg Philipp Telemann Musikalische Werke.*

53. *Johann Sebastian Bach: Neue Ausgabe sämtlicher Werke*, except for vocal slurs, which are from Bach's autograph manuscript.

54. *Johann Sebastian Bach: Neue Ausgabe sämtlicher Werke*, except for vocal slurs, which are from Bach's autograph manuscript.

55. Christ Church College, Oxford, Mus. MS 14.

56. Fitzwilliam Museum, Cambridge, MS 88.

57. *Hallische Händel-Ausgabe.*

58. *Forty Select Anthems* (1743).

59. *Libro de Coro XV*, Pueblo Cathedral.

60. *Archivo Musica Sacra Cat. Met. C: de Mex.* [Mexico City Cathedral].

61. Haydn's self-engraved score of 1800, with the addition of articulation marks found in early sets of orchestral parts and noted in A. Peter Brown's 1991 Oxford edition of the oratorio. Vocal slurs are in accordance with the English text.

62. *Salve Regina*, MH634 (1796).

63. *Neue Mozart-Ausgabe.*

64. *Franz Schubert: Neue Ausgabe sämtliche Werke.*

65. Mozart autograph manuscript, Süssmayr autograph manuscript, and the *Neue Mozart-Ausgabe.* Slurring marks are based on the autograph manuscripts.

66. Revised second version (1841), published by B. Schott fils (1842).

67. *The Singing Master's Assistant* (1782).

68. *Hector Berlioz: New Edition of the Complete Works* (1979) and *Hector Berlioz: Werke* (1901).

69. *Deux choeurs* (1882).

70. Fauré manuscript Ms. 412, Bibliothèque Nationale (1888) and the Nectoux-Delage edition, published by Hamelle (1994).

71. Verdi's autograph score, with slurring consistencies based on the 1990 David Rosen edition, published by the University of Chicago Press.

72. *Ludwig van Beethovens Werke* and Beethoven's autograph manuscript.

73. *Felix Mendelssohn-Bartholdys Werke* and the 2009 Douglass Seaton edition of *Elijah*, published by Bärenreiter.

74. *Robert Schumann's Werke.*

75. *Franz Listzs musikalische Werke.*

76. *Anton Bruckner: Gesamtausgabe.*

77. First edition, J. Rieter-Bidermann (1868) and *Johannes Brahms: Neue Ausgabe sämtlicher Werke*, with expressive annotations found in the Reimenschneider Bach Institute, "A Recently Discovered Composer-Annotated Score of the Brahms *Requiem*."

78. *Johannes Brahms: Neue Ausgabe sämtlicher Werke.*

79. *Abendlied*, op. 69 no. 3 (1873).

80. *Antonín Dvořák: Souborné vydání.*

81. *Four Sacred Choruses from the Liturgy of St. John Chrysostom* (1897).

82. *Vsenoshchnoye bdeniye (All-Night Vigil)*, op. 59 (1912).

83. *Ten Communion Hymns*, op. 25 no. 10.

84. *Vsenoshchnoye bdeniye (All-Night Vigil)*, op. 37 no. 6 (1915).

85. *My Soul, There Is a Country* (1916).

86. First publication by Boosey and Hawkes (1905).

87. *Scenes from the Saga of King Olaf*, op. 30 (1896).

88. *The Sabbath Hymn and Tune Book* (1859).

89. *Two Northern Songs*, op. 43, published by Arthur P. Schmidt (1891).

90. *Through the House Give Glimmering Light*, published by Arthur P. Schmidt (1897).

91. Bibliothéque nationale, Paris, MS 192.

92. Editions Durand & Cie, Paris (1916).

93. Facsimile of the autograph manuscript, which differs from the published score in a number of respects: tenuto markings; syllabic as well as longer phrasing slurs (marked only above the soprano parts); additional *messa di voce* signs (measures 14, 33, and 27); and textual punctuation.

94. Première version (1921), published by Foetisch Frères S.A. (1924–25).

95. *Vieille prière bouddhique*, published Durand & Cie, Paris (1921).

96. Copyright Éditions Salabert. With the kind authorization of Les Éditions Salabert.

97. Copyright 1948 Éditions Durand S. A. With the kind authorization of Les Éditions Salabert.

98. Copyright 1926 by Universal Edition A. G., Wien. © Renewed. All rights reserved. Used by permission of European American Music Distributors LLC.

99. Universal Edition (1921).

Composer Index

CPSIA information can be obtained
at www.ICGtesting.com
Printed in the USA
BVHW060721090122
625107BV00002B/8